# The Extraordinary presence of GOD

## True Stories of Faith and Courage in Ordinary Lives

## Ann White Knowles

*The Extraordinary Presence of God*

© 2020, 2015 Ann White Knowles

Paperback ISBN-13: 978-1-948026-53-6
Hardcover ISBN-13: 978-1-948026-60-4
Digital ISBN-13: 978-1-948026-54-3

Unless otherwise noted, Scriptures are taken from the Holy Bible, New International Version®, NIV®. Copyright © 1973, 1978, 1984, 2011 by Biblica, Inc.™ Used by permission of Zondervan. All rights reserved worldwide. **www.zondervan.com.**

Scripture quotations marked "KJV" are from the King James Version by public domain.

Scripture quotations marked "NKJV" are taken from The New King James Version / Thomas Nelson Publishers, Nashville: Thomas Nelson Publishers., Copyright © 1982. Used by permission. All rights reserved.

Scripture quotations marked "HCSB" are taken from the Holman Christian Standard Bible (HCSB) Copyright © 1999, 2000, 2002, 2003, 2009 by Holman Bible Publishers, Nashville, Tennessee. All rights reserved.

Published by TMP Books, 3 Central Plaza Ste 307, Rome, GA 30161

www.TMPBooks.com

# Table of Contents

# Dedication

To the Awesome God we serve

*Great is the Lord, and greatly to be praised; And His greatness is unsearchable. One generation shall praise Your works to another, And shall declare Your mighty acts.*

Ps. 145:3, 4 (NKJV)

Royalties from this book are dedicated to
Christ to the World Ministries

# Christist to the World Ministries

*(From their website: www.ChristToTheWorld.com, reprinted with permission)*

## Our Mission

Our mission is to honor and carry out the final command of our Lord and Savior, Jesus Christ, to "Go and make disciples of all nations" (Matt. 28:19).We focus on bringing people to a saving knowledge of and faith in Jesus Christ as Savior and Lord. We do this through dramas and Bible studies that present the message of the Bible and the story of Jesus in ways that people everywhere can understand and relate to. These programs are translated into thirty-two languages and broadcast in fifty countries around the world.

## Our Vision

Our vision is to see that "great multitude that no one could count, from every nation, tribe, people and language, standing before the throne and in front of the Lamb" (Rev. 7:9) and to know that CTTW was used by God to add to that number.

The great need of our day is to present the saving message of Jesus to a lost and dying world. That message is contained in the Bible, God's Word. Jesus said: *"Heaven and earth will pass away, but my words will never pass away"* (Mark 13:31). The prophet of old declared, *the grass withers, and the flowers fall, but the word of our God stands forever"* (Isa. 40:8). When the mighty empires of the world have crumbled and turned into dust, God's Word will remain.

If you are a writer who desires to reach lost people for Christ, CTTW Ministries invites you to write for them. Contact annknowles03@aol.com for information and workshops on writing Biblical Radio Dramas and Bible Study Scripts or request Ann at your next writer's conference.

# ACKNOWLEDGEMENTS

When *The Extraordinary Presence of God* was returned to me by the first publisher, I contacted my dear friend Tracy Ruckman, author, editor, and publisher. We still believed every story would touch someone's heart. She readily accepted the challenge of publishing this 2nd Edition. The amazing thing is she wanted to do it as a labor of love for the Lord and for me. Without Tracy on our side, our book would have died.

We could not contact some of our writers because they had moved or changed email addresses, but Tracy patiently worked to update as many stories as possible.

I owe this book to her expertise and faithful obedience to the leadership of the Holy Spirit. With all my heart, I say, "Thank you, Tracy, for making this possible."

# Introduction

People who believe Jesus is the same yesterday, today, and forever submitted the stories in this book. He was present when the world was created and then later came to earth to live among men and to die for our sins. Today He lives in the hearts of believers. So why would He not perform miracles today?

What seems like a miracle to us isn't really a miracle to God. He can do anything, and in reality, He is busy performing miracles all around us all the time. Some of us acknowledge them and others fail to see God at work in their lives. As you will see from the stories in this book, our authors believe that only God has the power to perform miracles, but He may sometimes choose to use others in His work. You will read accounts of God's extraordinary presence in the lives of ordinary people. Many believe His presence is miraculous, whether it is a life-saving event, or the subtle presence of a helping hand when we cannot accomplish a task on our own, or when a whispered prayer is answered.

# Our Special Child

## by Claudia Russell

I am the mother of a very special son named Scott, who was born in 1971. He was the second son born to my husband and me. The morning after his birth, we learned he had two problems: his feet were turned in and would require casting, and he had pneumonia. They placed him in an incubator and started him on antibiotics.

Although he was born on a Thursday evening, I did not get to see him or hold him until Saturday morning. At six pounds three ounces, he was three pounds lighter than my first child and looked and felt so very tiny to me. When the nurse brought him to me Saturday morning, she said I had a very special child who would need lots of love and care. The doctor planned to send me home on Monday, but Scott would remain in the hospital a little longer.

We lived an hour's drive from the hospital and the doctor said not to come back until he called us. Every day the hospital sent a progress report, and on Thursday, they told us we could bring him home.

Scott required lots of love and attention. He had some difficulty breathing and swallowing at the same time, which caused him to get strangled often. He would take in less than an ounce of formula per feeding and would fall back to sleep. The hospital set us up an orthopedic appointment for him when he was three weeks old. We traveled two hours to the orthopedic office. They put casts on both his feet, and we began semi-weekly trips to the orthopedic doctors.

The same week that Scott had his first cast, he began to spit up a lot. Each day it seemed to get worse. I took him to our family doctor and he changed his formula twice. By then he was not only spitting up; he forcefully threw-up. The doctor admitted him to the hospital. X-rays revealed that he had pyloric stenosis. The muscle at the end of his stomach was contracted and would not allow his food to pass through.

The doctor sent us to a hospital another half hour away from our home. By that time, Scott was five weeks old and weighed just five pounds, with casts on both feet. He was so tiny that we could have pulled his feet right out of the casts. The doctor decided to give him fluids overnight and do the corrective surgery the next morning.

I thought he might have to catch up developmentally with all he had been through. At four months, he still could not hold his head up very well and he constantly struggled to breath. His breathing was noisy. The doctor assured me that all babies were different and that he just needed more time and all would be well.

When Scott was five months old, we moved from the coast to the mountains of NC. We had been there only a couple of weeks and I had not yet found a new doctor for our boys. One Sunday afternoon, Scott was crying and when I changed his diaper, I discovered a large inguinal hernia. We took him to the emergency room and the doctor on duty told us he didn't think Scott could survive the surgery. They called in a pediatrician who scheduled him for an office appointment the next morning.

When we arrived at the pediatric office, both of the pediatricians came into the exam room. They looked Scott over with a fine-toothed comb. They kept saying things like "He looks mosaic" and they traced the lines in his hands. I was totally confused about what all this meant. Finally, they said they wanted us to go to the genetic clinic for testing. As long as the hernia could be suppressed, they didn't want to have him go through any more surgery at this time. They scheduled Scott for an appointment the next week at the genetic clinic in Chapel Hill, NC.

The day of our appointment at Chapel Hill began early and when we arrived at the clinic, a wonderful supportive staff met us and gave us a bassinet for Scott along with all the supplies we would need for the day. We saw many doctors along with the teams they were teaching. The medical staff performed blood tests, urine tests, x-rays, and a developmental evaluation. Five or six different specialists examined Scott and at the end of the day, our head doctor talked to us about their findings. Scott's liver and spleen were enlarged, he had a heart murmur, and his breathing passages were very small. As we talked, a technician came to the room and the two of them went outside to discuss Scott's case.

The doctor came back in, excused himself, and promised he would be right back. When he returned he said that one of the tests had been run three times to rule out any error and that he then ran the test two additional times himself and it was positive each time. He wept as he told us that Scott had a very rare chemical disorder that was life threatening; there was no way he could live to be two years old. As much as he wanted to give us better news, there was no cure, nothing could be done.

The news was devastating, but his next suggestion was what really left us speechless.

"Be kind to yourselves, as well as your older child, and leave Scott here with us. We'll place him in a special unit for dying babies and we'll let you know when it is over."

Heartbroken and tears streaming down my face, I shook my head. "No sir. I can't do that. I can't just hand over my son to you and leave him here to die."

The doctor suggested we take him home for three months. Perhaps by then, we'd be ready to let him go.

When Scott was six months old, he had only turned over once when he was struggling. He paid no attention to the small rattle or other toys I left in his crib. He didn't smile at us or do any of the things other babies his age were doing. Our home was a very sad place.

I knew that God has a plan for our lives before we are ever born. I prayed often for Scott, pouring my heart out to God. "Please, God, I know without a doubt that You are almighty; that you have all power in heaven and in earth. Please, God, heal our son."

Winter came and so did the colds and congestion that follow. Scott's breathing problems intensified; you could hear him wheezing all over the house. I struggled with how to pray and questioned why God wasn't answering my prayers as I wanted Him to. I changed my way of praying. "Lord, I can accept that you may heal him by taking him to be with you. I surrender him totally to you, but if he dies, he dies in my arms not someone else's."

On December 13, 1971, I was reading a story to our older son as Scott was napping in his room, when I heard one of the little rattles I always left in his bed. Scott had never reached for one or played with it in anyway. When went to his room, we discovered he had turned himself over and was holding the rattle looking at it. When I spoke to him, he smiled up at me. It was as if he had awakened for the first time. That Christmas was so wonderful. Scott was much better, and we were all so happy.

When we went back to Chapel Hill the first week of January, the doctors could not believe how well he was doing. They all checked him over again. His liver was no longer enlarged, his heart murmur was only superficial, his body was gaining strength and weight, and his breathing problems were much improved. However, the best part was that they ran the same test over again and found that the rare chemical disorder was no longer present. They ran the test multiple times just as before and it was just not there. The doctor was almost as happy as we were. He assured us that this was not anything man did; only Almighty God could have healed Scott of this problem.

Scott has faced other challenges in his 43 years, but I know without a doubt that God healed him of the life-threatening disorder.

# UPDATE:

For a precious little boy whose parents were told he would not live to be two, he is now about to turn 49. Scott still loves his church and never sees a stranger. He is such an ambassador for the Lord. Scott tells people that Jesus loves them. His best friend is his little dog, Lady, and he spends much time with her. He also loves to help our neighbors with yard work and just to love on them. He still often tells me how much he longs to see Jesus and how he wants to thank Him for life, love and salvation. He says the first thing he wants to do when he gets to heaven is to kiss Jesus' feet. Oh, how much he humbles me, and blesses my life and the life of all those he encounters.

# An Angel in Black Scrubs

## by Eva Marie Everson

When my cell phone rang with my son-in-law's name on the screen, I answered with my usual, "Hey, Tony!" He, my daughter, and my grandson—Vonché, age twenty-months—were expected soon for dinner, which simmered on the stove.

But, instead of his typical, "Hey, Mom!" and what I expected (something like, "We're leaving in a minute."), his sobs met my ears. "He's not breathing! He's not breathing!" he wailed.

"Who?" I asked, although my heart knew he meant my grandson, their miracle baby.

"The baby! Oh, God … Oh, God …"

My daughter's voice came on next. "Mother, we're on our way to the medical center down the street from our house," she said. Her voice held a strange mixture of stress and calm.

My old nurse's training and work rose to the surface. "Tell me exactly what's happening."

"I don't know," she said, now weeping. "He had a seizure. He *is* breathing, but it's shallow."

"Why didn't you call 9-1-1?" I asked.

"It's closer. Easier. I'll call you back."

And the line went dead.

I told my husband the news, then went to the stove to stir a pot of beans, mainly—I believe—because I was in a state of shock. But before I could pick up the spoon, the Holy Spirit whispered, "Get in the car. Go." I looked at my husband. "I have to go," I said. "This isn't good." I gave him brief instructions on what to do with the meal. "I'll call you," I said as I dashed toward the garage.

I took off, heading … I wasn't sure where. More than *one* medical center existed near my daughter's home; I picked up my cell phone and dialed her number.

The call went to voice mail.

I called my son-in-law's number.

It also went to voice mail.

I tried my daughter again, each call being made at red lights and the travel in between feeling like a lifetime rather than a matter of seconds or minutes. Still, no answer.

I drove to one center, then another, then back to the first, continuing to call both numbers but to no avail. By then, I was making deals with God, begging … pleading. Unashamed. Then, as I felt ready to give up, my phone rang.

"Mom." Tony's voice was breathless.

"Tony, what's going on?"

"The ambulance took Vonché and Jessica to Arnold Palmer Children's Hospital. Can you come get me? I'm at the house with the car."

Their house was less than a mile away. I drove, praying out loud. "God, please don't take our baby boy. Please don't. I can't ... I can't go through this. Whatever you want me to do ... whatever you say ... just please let him be okay."

I knew God heard me and I knew he understood my anguish. If we lost this precious child, it would not be our first heartbreaking loss. Yet, this would be worse. Vonché had been our ticket back from the nightmare.

*He's going to be okay ...*

The voice came from nowhere, speaking deeply into my spirit.

*Say it. Say, "He's going to be okay."*

"He's going to be okay," I said. "He's going to be okay."

I pulled up in front of the two-story stucco home; Tony stood in front. He immediately got into my car, stricken. "Vonché! Vonché!" he cried.

"Tony," I said firmly. "Listen to me. He's going to be okay. He's going to grow up to be a mighty man of God. Say that. Say that with me."

"...mighty man of God," he whimpered.

"Now, listen," I said as I drove out of the neighborhood. "I don't have any idea where Arnold Palmer is. You *have* to get on your phone, get on Google Maps, and direct me."

For the next forty-five minutes or more, Tony and I drove through Orlando's busy streets during rush hour traffic.

Sometimes Tony cried. Sometimes he gave me directions. But always he answered Jessica's calls.

"He's not breathing on his own," she told us through the phone's speaker. "They've intubated him, but he never lost oxygen."

Tony cried all the harder. "No. No. That's good," I told him, grabbing his arm. "He's *going* to be okay."

Jessica continued, "He's in a coma and he's had several seizures." She took a shaky breath. "I heard them in the back of the ambulance say that he crashed."

"But he's alive," I said.

"Yes," she said.

We ended the call, still creeping along in the bumper-to-bumper traffic. I called my husband and told him he needed to "come to the hospital."

Tony and I neared the hospital; the only way I knew was by the number of ambulance sirens I heard. Google Maps could not account for the new construction in the area nor could it tell me *which* of the three hospitals of the Orlando Regional Medical Center I should park near. Arnold Palmer Children's Hospital, ORMC, or Winnie Palmer Women's Hospital. "Tony," I said, pulling into an open parking place, "When we get inside, start looking for the emergency room."

We got out, locked the doors, and took off running for the glass doors. As soon as we exited the hot August heat for the air-conditioning of the hospital, we looked for signs pointing to our destination. We found them and made our way quickly down the hallways only to be met by a security guard standing next to the double-doors leading to where we believed the baby fought for his life. "Can I help you?" he asked.

"We're looking for his son," I said, pointing to Tony. "My grandson. We were told he is here."

"How old is your grandson?" The question didn't come from the security guard, but from a man standing behind Tony. A man I hadn't seen only a second before when I'd indicated Tony to the guard, but who clearly stood there now. He was young, dark-haired, and he wore scrubs.

"Twenty-months," Tony said.

"You're in the wrong hospital," the man said. "Hold on a second."

He disappeared behind the double-doors. I looked at the guard who seemed puzzled. "I guess he knows something I don't," he said.

Before I could reply, the dark-haired young man reappeared and said, "Follow me."

Tony was able to match his steps while mine fell behind. He led us out of the hospital, weaving us between thick buildings where steam rose from huge air-conditioning compressors, one block after the other. I could hear Tony telling our story, but I couldn't make out what the young man had to say in return. Worse, in the back of my mind, I kept wondering *how* the man knew where Vonché was being treated.

We neared another set of glass doors. "Here you go," the man said, stopping. "Through those doors there is where you want to go."

He turned and, for the first time, I saw the hospital security badge clipped to his scrub's shirt pocket. DOCTOR.

That was it. No name. No location of department. Simply: DOCTOR.

My old training returned as he stepped past me, back toward where we'd begun. *Doctors* don't stop what they are doing to walk people through an enormous complex of buildings nearly three city blocks away. *Especially young emergency room doctors.* Probably, in fact, a resident. Or an intern. *They simply don't. And since when do doctors wear black scrubs? Or only have* DOCTOR *on their ID badges?*

I turned around to call out a "thank you" to the young man I believed had gone beyond what he *had* to do. The young man who fit absolutely no description of any doctor—intern, resident, whatever—I'd ever known.

But he was gone. Simply … gone.

Although Vonché had somewhere between six and eight seizures, the cause was never determined. He remained in a coma until the following day and for about three days, stayed in what I believe is the finest children's hospital in the nation. When he returned to us, he opened his dark eyes with new wisdom. We don't know what happened or why, but we do know two things: 1) He *is* okay. In fact, he is amazing and, we've been told, now demonstrating "gifted child" mentality; and 2) a man in black scrubs guided us to a location that, I believe, it may have taken us another hour to find had we been left on our own. A critical hour.

An hour we could never have gotten back.

To this day, Tony and I both believe we came face to face with someone—something—other than a doctor. Perhaps, we think, an angel "unaware."

We may never know and, in all honesty, it doesn't matter. What does matter is that God heard. He is faithful. He is good!

# UPDATE:

The most amazing thing happened after my grandson came out of his coma. Within a week, at only 18 months, he spoke in complete sentences (he had not done this before). He knew his alphabet front to back, back to front, and could recite it phonetically as well. Shortly after this, he could read, not only English but also Hebrew. There is no doubt in our minds that his sudden abilities were due to whatever happened to his brain during those awful hours.

Today he is seven years old and in school where he takes advanced classes, some two years ahead of his age group. He is a godly boy, which is the most important thing to all of us. Sweet, talented, funny, and definitely Jesus' boy!

# God's Perfect Plan

### by Natalie Driggs

Our adoption journey is a testimony about trusting God.
Adoption is a roller coaster ride with ups, downs, and curves.
God laid it on our family's heart to adopt long before we
started the process. During that time, we prayed as a family and
in our quiet times alone with God. We knew He was leading us
to China. But when? And how?

Four years went by. The desire in my heart grew stronger
each day. I read blogs of others' adoptions. Sometimes, in
tears, I would read them to my family. Then on Valentine's
Day, my husband presented me with a blank check to start the
process. It would be a leap of faith because we didn't have the
money to adopt, but God knew our needs.

The paper chase began. There was a lot of paperwork to
do in order to collect all the information for our Chinese
adoption. The roller coaster ride began, and it was at that point,
I made a decision. No matter what, I would choose to trust
God. It all belonged to Him: our daughter, the money, the
whole process. It was all His.

The first bump came during our adoption home study
when the social worker did not meet her deadlines. This pushed

the adoption date further away. Some doctors were unwilling to take time to notarize papers; the notary's license was close to expiring.

All this cost us precious time and money because we had to re-do things. The social worker's mistake alone cost us a thousand dollars.

For our Chinese adoption, we requested a little girl birth to four years old. On Mother's Day weekend, a year after starting the paper chase, we got a call from our agency.

"We have a little girl for you to look at. She fits all of your requests and the special need that you said you were willing to accept, but she will be a little older than you requested. By the time you travel, she will be five years old. Her name is Wen Li."

We had asked for a younger child, but I wanted to trust God and not second-guess our decision when it came to finding the right daughter for our family. Therefore, I never allowed myself to get caught up looking at the monthly lists of available children sent to us by the agency. I wanted to know with certainty that God had picked out the child that was best for our family.

When we received the call about Wen Li, I took all her paperwork to our pediatrician to evaluate her health issues. We discussed her special need, Hepatitis B, but the doctor really couldn't conclude anything from her file. Based on the levels in her blood work, the numbers were high; however, Chinese charts are not the same as American charts, so it was hard to determine the level of her need. The doctor gave me nothing to go on. Just before I left her office, she stopped me, took the photo of Wen Li, and studied it. She asked if this was recent. I said, "I think so, but I'm not sure."

Then the doctor's statement got my attention, "She sure has pink cheeks and a healthy look to her skin and eyes. If her numbers were as high as they say, she would be jaundiced and those cheeks are too pink, plus her urine says no bilirubin." That was the moment I knew that God had chosen Wen Li to be our daughter.

We had a family meeting and I said, "I know she's the one," but my husband Chris said he needed more time to pray about it. After a few days, he was sure Wen Li was definitely the little girl for us. We called the agency.

God's timing was perfect, if our adoption home study had concluded earlier, our dossier would have arrived in China earlier and we probably would have missed her. But God knew all about Wen Li and about our family.

On the flight to China, as we flew over the North Pole, God spoke again and said, " Do you realize you started praying for your daughter five years ago and when you finally get to hold her in your arms and speak loving words to her, she will be five years old?" God had picked out the perfect child for our family long before she was born. God reminded me that He did have it all in His hands.

Wen Li is from the Hunan Province of China. The females from the Hunan Province are called "Spicy Girls" because everyone there eats spicy food and the girls have spicy personalities. She fits that to a tee. She has two older brothers, our sons Joshua and Alex, and she can hold her own with them any day. God matched them up just right, two brothers and a spicy little sister.

Today Wen Li is ten years old and is in good health. Her blood reports first came back as a carrier of Hepatitis B, but each year her levels have dropped and now there is no trace of it in her body. The fact that she no longer carries Hepatitis B is another miracle in our adoption journey.

Wen Li attends a Christian school where she has learned many Bible stories and memorized numerous Scripture verses. She asked Jesus to be her Lord and Savior, and after Vacation Bible School last year, she was baptized.

God is faithful! We just have to trust Him.

# UPDATE:

Wen Li is fifteen years old now. She has grown into an amazing young woman. She has been with her forever family for ten years as of December 2019. In the past few years she has been baptized, went on her first international mission trip and returned to China for a visit. She is a junior at Wilmington

Christian Academy and volunteers at the hospital. She thinks she might like to be a nurse when she grows up.

For now, Wen Li focuses on things that are important to her. She works very hard at all her subjects and maintains a good academic average. She is well rounded, has lots of friends, loves messing around with her older brothers, does not like sports, and does not want to learn how to drive (in case you were wondering).

Ann White Knowles

# My Dukes of Hazzard Day

## by Lorna Bius

I remember watching *The Dukes of Hazzard* TV show as a kid. Good ole boys, Bo and Luke Duke, seemed to find all sorts of drama in their small county of Hazzard. Every week there were car chases and wrecks in the serene countryside. No matter how bad the car crash, everyone always walked away unharmed. I never could figure that out. Until one Sunday afternoon in late January.

I was excited that I was going to be driving through beautiful scenery in the west until I discovered a notorious winter storm was on its way. I say notorious because I live in the Denver area, and such storms are common. With that in mind, I decided to leave immediately after church, and head toward the conference I was to attend in Casper, Wyoming, hoping I could avoid the worst of the storm and darkness. Growing up in South Georgia, storms or darkness was not that big a deal, even in the winter. However, here in the west, brutal snow and ice storms can shut down entire interstates. And Wyoming is no exception.

While packing my car, I put my heaviest coat and my gloves in the back seat where I could easily reach them. As I drove north out of Denver on the well-traveled corridor of Interstate 25, I noticed the beautiful blue sky and white puffy clouds. I wondered when I would begin to see the changing weather that could not be far ahead.

Not long after crossing into the open beauty of Wyoming, the wind began to pick up, pushing hard against my non-aerodynamic SUV. As I continued on, the white clouds turned gray, and soon a light snow covered the ground. The concrete interstates below my vehicle seemed to turn into a mystical fog as the wind pushed the white confetti across my path in waves.

Just north of Cheyenne, I came up to what looked like a big cloud that had just decided to sit down on the road. As I approached it, the huge cloud completely enveloped me. I slowed down and turned on my emergency lights. The fog was so thick I could barely see beyond the hood of my SUV even though it was still daylight.

As I moved along cautiously through the fog, I saw the red and blue flashing lights of a State Trooper's vehicle, and then I saw a car that had apparently slid off the highway. Suddenly I was out of the cloud and into clear weather and open road. Thank God, I was now out of danger. Driving with caution, I began to pick up speed. Ahead of me, the driving conditions looked much better.

Suddenly, my SUV began to slide. I had no control. *Stay calm. Don't brake!* My sliding vehicle turned suddenly into a jolting thunderous crash. Panic gripped me. I remember thinking *Oh, no! I'm flipping over! Please, God, help me.* It happened so quickly that I had little time to think of what might happen next.

After several flips, the truck came to a rest on its side. The wind blowing in through broken windows was the only sound I heard. I put my hand up to my face, felt my head, and looked at my arms and legs. There were no visible injuries. I took a deep breath and said aloud, "Thank You, Lord, for protecting me."

Two cars behind me stopped, and the men ran towards me. They yelled, "Are you okay?" as they peered in through my open windshield.

"Yes, I think I'm fine" I replied. "I just need help getting out."

The men helped me crawl through the windshield. I now was standing by my mangled truck in the freezing Wyoming wind. *"Where's that jacket? And where is my phone?"*

I pulled my jacket, now ripped and dirty, through the broken window. I put in on and began looking for my phone. It was nowhere to be found.

The ambulance arrived and the EMT checked me out, confirming that there were no injuries except a bruise on my shoulder and a few aches. As I sat on the bench in the back of the ambulance, my heart sank as I thought about my family. What if they heard about my accident on the news? I couldn't call them; my phone was gone.

I had always named my cars, and on that cold, January day, as I peered out the ambulance window at Grace, a mangled mess of metal, broken glass, and scratched paint lying on its side. I realized it had earned its name, for it was a true depiction of Grace—God's unmerited love, even when we are a wreck.

I caught a ride with the tow truck driver who took me to a small motel in Wheatland, WY. A kind employee allowed me to use her cell phone to call my Dad and sister.

The next morning a very gracious lady drove me to Casper, where I joined the conference I was to attend.

There are many stories involved in this unexpected turn of events, but the main thing about my story is the Lord's love and peace that covered me every moment. His fingerprints were on every detail. He was watching over me that day in spite of the accident, He kept me safe and provided everything I needed. God's mercy and the prayers of loved ones far away ministered to me in miraculous ways. Somehow, God manifests His love and the love of others to us just when we need it most.

While Grace the car is gone, God's grace is more precious to me than ever. Job 10:12 says it best, "You gave me life and faithful love, and Your care has guarded my life." Truly, He had guarded my life.

# Life Is a Miracle

## by Rebecca F. DePra

There are people who call it "luck" when good things happen. If that were true, I'd be the luckiest girl on the planet because my life has been a festival of miracles. There is no such thing as luck when we know and acknowledge that we have a mighty God who has ordained the days of our lives here on earth to bring Him honor and glory. Through the gifts He has given to each of us and the plans he has for each life, He is able to accomplish miraculous things. Sometimes the miracles are major events of divine intervention and sometimes they are subtle things that let us know He is there when we need Him most.

My mother told me about the first miracle in my life. She was about to have a miscarriage. I was already in the birth process, when a woman came to my mother's aid. She placed her hands on my mother's very pregnant belly and prayed, asking God to stop the miscarriage and save the baby. When the doctor arrived, he was stunned that the miscarriage had stopped and he kneaded me safely back in place. I came into the world, a healthy baby girl, at the appointed time.

Another miracle involved a family trip to the beach. We were having a great time playing in the surf. We didn't go far because I couldn't swim and my sister and brother could only swim a little. Although we knew about dangerous undercurrents that could unexpectedly pull a person out without warning, we suddenly found ourselves in deep water, and we were being pulled farther out. I remember crying for help and seeing my father trying to get us to safety. The next thing I remember was being held by a muscular man with light brown skin, I never saw his face; he was holding me in the crook of his arm the same way a football player holds the ball when running through a host of tacklers. With the other hand, the man was pulling my father along. He put me down on the sand and let go of my father's hand. My father collapsed on the beach. I thought he was dead and with great anxiety, I cried out "Papi, Papi." He waved his hand to let me know he was okay, but lay there exhausted. I turned to thank the man, but he was nowhere to be seen. Nobody nearby resembled the man who had rescued us. My parents said God had sent an angel to save us.

God brought my family from Puerto Rico to the United States and opened the door for me to study in Philadelphia at Temple University. An amazing thing happened one day as I was on my way to class to take an important test. I was running a bit late and decided I'd jay-walk before the light turned green. Just as I made a run for the other side to catch the school shuttle, a woman decided to move to the left lane and turn. Her car struck my leg; the momentum of the impact sent me headfirst to the pavement and put me in an uncontrollable spin.

Since I was near Temple University Hospital, an ambulance arrived quickly and whisked me away to the emergency room. When the doctor in the ER checked me, I didn't have a concussion, not even a bump on my head. My leg was not broken, but I did have a hematoma the size of a grapefruit and a few scrapes and bruises. The man I would one day marry was a fourth-year medical student doing a rotation at the emergency room. He discharged me, and a few days later, I met him again—and again and again. Two years later we were married—twenty-six years ago. What a way to meet the love of my life!

A few years after marriage our family began to grow with the arrival of our first born of three. I think learning to parent requires some miracles in most cases because young parents simply aren't knowledgeable enough or wise enough to know how to handle all kinds of circumstances that children place us in. I had my share of small miracles. One was when I missed a step and started to fall backward, holding our baby boy. God literally sent an angel to push me forward and kept the baby and me from harm. Our middle child jumped off the diving board as a toddler. As I ran to catch him, he took off swimming. And another time was when I was changing my baby girl on top of the washing machine; I reached to grab a baby wipe and she rolled off and fell on the tile floor. God must have put a natural helmet on her head because she suffered no injury.

My latest miracle happened two years ago when God spared my life once more as a blood clot formed, but never made it to my brain. I was on blood thinners and the doctor put a tiny camera down to my heart to see what was going on there. He found three smaller blood clots. If any of the clots had gone to my lungs, heart, or brain, there could have been irreparable damage. Instead, medication dissolved the small clots and the larger one went south to my kidney.

The doctor told me I was "blessed." Most doctors will say "blessed" when they know luck just doesn't account for the miracle they witnessed. My damaged kidney is fully recovered, and despite a pacemaker at forty-eight, I am still practicing Tae Kwando with a Christian twist (no mumbo, jumbo, here).

The "good luck" that occurs in one's life is simply a result of the unending love that is expressed by our heavenly Father. We call it a miracle!

# The Surgeon's Hands

## by Rebecca Floyd

It was the spring of 2010 and our two-year-old son Franklin was scheduled for a double nephrectomy in two days. Our hearts were troubled with constant thoughts and feelings about how losing both kidneys would affect Franklin's long-term survival. Just three months prior, Franklin had been diagnosed with bilateral Wilms Tumor (a rare cancer of the kidneys that primarily affects children under the age of six). He had undergone three months of chemotherapy and a biopsy of the tumors on both kidneys. We were at a crossroads in the cancer treatment. Dr. Gold, his oncologist, advised that this was the time to remove any remaining tumor and proceed with more chemo and radiation therapy.

Previously Franklin's medical team had been hopeful that enough of one or both of his kidneys would be sufficient to sustain him without the aid of dialysis or kidney transplant. However, diagnostic testing of the kidney function and tumor position indicated that the possibility of salvaging any usable kidney tissue was slim to none. Franklin's surgeon, Dr. Sutherland, at UNC Children's Hospital in Chapel Hill, NC told us, "Almost all of Franklin's kidney function is coming from the kidney with the smaller tumor, but the renal artery is a mere millimeter away from the tumor, rendering it nearly impossible to remove the tumor without destroying this vital artery."

We faced the reality of destroying our son's cancer, and in the process, a vital artery as well. Kidney transplant was not a viable option at the time.

Our medical team advised us to proceed with surgery to remove both of Franklin's kidneys. My husband and I were beside ourselves with shock and fear as we arranged for the surgery. I could think of nothing else, and I could not stop crying.

We had been reaching out to God, pleading for wisdom, strength, and healing since the beginning of our ordeal. An amazing team of prayer warriors from around the world was praying for Franklin.

As we drove home from the hospital, we checked e-mails from our phone. One in particular stood out because it was from a woman we did not know.

"Have you checked with Dr. LaQuaglia at Sloan Kettering, he is known for saving kidneys?"

At the time, Dave and I were in the middle of trying to accept the fate of our little boy. We contemplated the possibility of better options while the logical part of our minds warned us of the futility of such thoughts.

Once we arrived home, I went straight to the internet and looked up Dr. LaQuaglia at Memorial Sloan Kettering cancer hospital in New York City. His bio indicted that he handled cases like Franklin's regularly. Still, Franklin's case was unique. It seemed futile to think that he could actually help our child. Despite the logical part of my mind telling me "No," with trembling hands, I dialed the number to Dr. LaQuaglia's office. I felt ridiculous as I explained to Dr. LaQuaglia's assistant that my son had bilateral Wilms Tumor and was scheduled for a double nephrectomy in two days. Further, I stated, "I have heard that Dr. LaQuaglia is good at saving kidneys." The assistant, Sarah, was very kind and patient; she affirmed that Dr. LaQuaglia was indeed highly qualified to remove kidney tumors. She insisted that I have Franklin's latest CT scans overnighted to their office. She promised she would make sure Dr. LaQuaglia took a look at them.

Late in the afternoon the following day, we received a phone call from Dr. LaQuaglia's office, "The doctor looked at the scans and feels he can save most of Franklin's right kidney." We were too stunned to speak. We couldn't believe there was actually hope that one of Franklin's kidneys might be spared.

Dr. LaQuaglia spoke with Dr. Sutherland and they both decided we should go to New York City and have Franklin's surgery done there.

David's Aunt Linda had come from Ohio a week earlier to

lend a hand, and she was able to stay with our daughter Carolyn who was in first grade at the time.

The next morning, we flew from North Carolina to New York City. On Friday afternoon we were in Dr. LaQuaglia's office for Franklin's pre-op. Surgery was scheduled for the following Monday.

Another parent in the children's oncology waiting area told us "Dr. LaQuaglia is the best. He did the surgery on our son's brain tumor. He is not only a good surgeon, but also a strong Christian. He prays before he operates." We were comforted by the fact that he was in the skilled hands of one of God's own surgeons.

The day of the surgery came with much anticipation, but also lots of anxiety. The medical team took Franklin to surgery and we waited from morning until evening. Finally, we were ushered into a windowless, private room, where Dr. LaQuaglia eventually came in, still dressed in scrubs, and said, "I saved over 90% of the right kidney and he is doing well and making urine."

Dr. LaQuaglia not only removed all visible tumor, he was also miraculously able to save Franklin's renal artery. We had just witnessed a true God-given miracle. Over 90% of a kidney was beyond anything we had hoped for.

Dave and I were both amazed at how God had worked this out—from the time Aunt Linda showed up until the doctor announced the positive results of the surgery. We were overwhelmed with emotion; tears flowed unchecked.

Franklin's renal surgery was about four and a half years ago as I write this. There has been no cancer recurrence in the right kidney and no need for dialysis. He just celebrated his seventh birthday and began first grade this year as an ordinary kid with no need for medical, social, or educational adaptations of any kind. Seeing him ride the school bus, climb monkey bars, play soccer and basketball—do everything other kids his age do—is so much more than we ever thought would be possible.

The journey through cancer treatments is long and arduous. But the greatest thing of all is the presence of God during times of darkness and hopelessness. Sometimes the message of hope and light can be as gentle as a whisper, a small kind gesture only large enough to erase a few of the cobwebs of despair, just enough to see the tiniest glimmer of light.

Our lives were changed forever by a seemingly benign act from a complete stranger who cared enough to e-mail us. There is no doubt; Franklin's life is a miracle.

# A Heart for Dancing

## by Phyllis Freeman

The audience at the 2007 Hotlanta's dance competition watched as a fifteen-year-old girl with flowing blond hair completed her performance of Paso Doble. The petite dancer in her scarlet red dress, a black flower in her hair, held her position as she received the audience's standing ovation. Amanda Freeman had melted their hearts.

Amanda won the overall Junior Ballroom Division that day. Neither the audience nor the judges knew that less than two years earlier, her life was in jeopardy from an internal predator.

As far back as second grade, Amanda wanted to run and play with other kids at recess. When she tried, she would dissolve in tears, telling her teacher, "I can't breathe very good," or "My heart is hurting." She did the same at family gatherings. So her mother would pull Amanda into her lap to snuggle and read to her.

Kyle and Sherry Freeman, Amanda's parents, from Chattanooga, TN were told repeatedly by a pediatrician that her problem was stress. Her mother thought, *What kind of stress can a child this age have?* They decided to enroll her in a

Christian school and allow her to repeat the third grade to lessen her anxiety.

Several times, the school called her parents to come and pick her up because she had episodes of illness. The school nurse called Amanda's dad one day, and told him she had blacked out during a class.

"Amanda's heart rate is exceptionally high. I recommend that you take her to a cardiologist."

They located a pediatric cardiologist but even with the medication he recommended, the symptoms continued and got worse. She weighed only forty-two pounds.

The pediatric cardiologist put Amanda on a heart monitor, which recorded an episode, and brought a diagnosis of Paroxysmal Supraventricular Tachycardia (PSVT). At times her heart rate accelerated to 200-250 beats per minute. The doctor explained to Kyle and Sherry that Amanda's arteries collected too much oxygen without providing the proper amount of blood supply to all her organs.

Because she weighed on forty-two pounds, the new doctor asked her parents if she was anorexic. The medication side effects—irritable bowel syndrome, upset stomach, and low blood sugar, affected her ability to gain weight. Her health continued to decline. She became claustrophobic in crowds, and landed in the emergency room every other month, yet no solutions.

One night, Amanda's mom found her lying on the floor in a fetal position. She was pale and her lips were gray—her blood pressure had bottomed out. Sherry rushed her to the emergency room, where they stabilized her with IV's. After that, Amanda's mom slept with her most of the time, afraid to leave her alone.

One night Sherry knelt beside the bed with Amanda and prayed, *God, I don't know how to help my little girl. Please help her.*

Amanda looked up at her mom and reached to wipe away her tears, saying, "Mommy, don't cry. I'll be okay. Jesus will take care of me."

Family members and others prayed regularly for Amanda, but there was no change. One day a friend slipped a piece of yellow paper into Sherry's hand saying, "You might want to check with this doctor in Atlanta. He specializes in adult cardio care, but maybe if he heard your story ..."

"If the doctor doesn't agree to take our case," Sherry said, "we'll accept that as God's answer." She called the specialist's office, and forty-five minutes later, her phone rang. The nurse asked for all of Amanda's medical records and set a date for a consultation.

Amanda weighed less than fifty pounds when her new cardiologist examined her. He spoke directly to her, "I'm basically a heart electrician. I can fix your heart, but you have to eat well and gain some weight. You need to weigh eighty-five pounds before I can safely perform the surgery to eliminate the short-circuiting of your heart's electrical system."

Amanda said later, "I remember thinking, what if I die in my sleep?" Yet, her faith was strong.

She told her parents not to worry, "Jesus is sleeping with me," she said. "Sometimes He sits on the foot of my bed."

The new medicines helped at first, but by the fall of 2005, when she turned thirteen, they were no longer working. She weighed only fifty-four pounds when she entered the seventh grade. The surgeon told her that by the next summer they should be able to do surgery.

Amanda looked in his eyes and said, "Doctor, I don't think my body will last until then."

"Ok then, during your Christmas school break we'll do it. How's that?"

By December, Amanda had gained a few more pounds, but she was still seventeen pounds less than the weight the doctor recommended for him to insert pediatric catheters into her tiny veins and to her heart.

The family traveled to Atlanta and stayed in a motel the night before surgery.

Kyle prayed, "Lord, you put Amanda in our care for thirteen years. Thank you for that. She's in your hands. If you decide to take her, please give us strength."

A still small voice spoke to Kyle, "Tell her, when she gets scared tomorrow to call out My name." As Amanda lay in the prep room the next morning, her daddy told her what God had said.

The surgical nurse later shared with the parents that when their fragile little girl began to feel sleepy with the anesthesia, she started her prayer, "Help me, Jesus; help me, Jesus; help me Jesus...."

Kyle and Sherry had to wait more than five hours for the surgery, much longer than they had anticipated. Finally, they saw the doctor walking toward them.

"Mom and Dad, Amanda is okay." The doctor then said, "But sit down, I have something to tell you"

"If you knew how these things work, this would blow your mind. I was totally unprepared for what I found. When the surgery had hardly begun, Amanda's heart went into voluntary tachycardia (racing), and then as I worked on her, she went into another. A few people with PSVT have a hidden second source of tachycardia. She did. It is called Wolff-Parkinson-White syndrome."

"I hesitated just a moment to consider my limited but urgent options. I knew the hidden WPW could take her heart up to 300-400 beats per minute putting her into cardiac arrest and heart failure."

"I needed to get to the other side of her heart to fix the WPW syndrome, but I knew I didn't have the pediatric material at hand to do another cath and I needed to act immediately."

"Then," he said, "I saw a small undiagnosed hole in her heart. All I can say, Mom and Dad, is that either it was missed by all her tests, or it appeared right then, because I had no idea her heart had a hole in it."

This statement brought real anxiety to them and it showed.

The doctor reassured them, "No, that was good. I realized that I could use this hole to get to the other side of the heart—it was just big enough.

"I don't know if you will believe me, but we were not alone in that operating room. Someone was watching over us."

About an hour after talking with the doctor, Kyle called me.

"Amanda came through the surgery fine, Mom." I knew his voice was cracking and that there was more to the story than he was telling me.

"What happened, Kyle?"

"Mom, I can't talk about it now, but it was a miracle," Kyle broke up and said he would call again later.

The next day the doctor checked Amanda thoroughly and released her. Everything was good to go.

The doctor now had a pet name for Amanda. "My Little Angel," he asked, "what do you want to do when you are completely recovered?"

Amanda did not hesitate, "I want to be a ballroom dancer."

Our family wanted Amanda's heart to be healed, but God had a bigger and better plan than we ever dreamed.

"Delight yourself also in the Lord, and He will give you the desires of your heart" Psalm 37:4 NKJV). He gave her the desire of her heart the night she danced the Paso Doble in Atlanta.

# Peace in the Midst of Suffering

## by Linda Harris

The summer sun beat down on the ambulance as I sat in the passenger seat praying. My husband and an EMT attended our sick three-year-old daughter, Joanna. I looked up at the cloudless sky and prayed for some relief from the heat, especially because I was four months pregnant with our son. We were on our way to Children's Hospital in Little Rock where Joanna would have a CAT scan.

I wrestled with all the uncertainties and questions that invaded my thoughts. *What if the tests at Children's Hospital show irreparable brain damage? Will all the stress I am under affect our unborn baby? Please, God, let Joanna be okay.* So many questions waited to be answered, and I pondered them as the ambulance sped along toward Little Rock.

It all started several days before when Joanna became ill while at a remote camp in Arkansas where my husband Bob and I were teaching young adults at a pre-conference retreat for our denomination. Just stepping outside the buildings brought a covering of mosquitoes, despite using copious amounts of insect repellant. The day we were scheduled to leave the camp,

Joanna woke up with a fever, chills, and what seemed to be convulsions.

Later that day a bus took us to Ouachita Baptist University in Arkadelphia. When we arrived, we requested someone take us to a doctor, but the members of the host committee were unable to arrange that.

The next morning someone provided transportation to the pediatrician's office in town. It didn't take Dr. Wesley Kluck long to diagnose dehydration, and he suspected meningitis or encephalitis, likely caused by all the mosquito bites Joanna had endured. He admitted her to the hospital in Arkadelphia.

They performed a spinal tap and when the results came back, she was diagnosed with both meningitis and encephalitis. It was unclear whether the infection was bacterial or viral. The doctors treated Joanna with antibiotics, with the hope it was bacterial.

While I remained in Joanna's room, Bob returned to the campus and immediately enlisted prayer from the conference attendees. Many called their home churches to put Joanna on their prayer chains. We suspect the prayers reached around the world as word spread of her illness.

Although the doctors said she wasn't in a coma, she was unconscious for several days. Dr. Kluck said we just needed to wait to see whether there would be any brain damage.

In the midst of IV pumps, alarms, and the business of the nurses going in and out her hospital room, God reminded me of a song: "My Peace I Give Unto You." Peace invaded the hospital room, despite what was happening around me. It was like God had given me a special blessing.

My husband insisted that I go back to the dormitory and get some rest. "I'll stay with Joanna while you sleep."

I reluctantly went to the dormitory, but being away from Joanna and the hospital removed the peace I had felt there. The next morning, I returned to the hospital to spend the nights where I could experience God's peace.

A few days later, Joanna opened her eyes, but didn't talk. We hoped for the best and prayed that she would return to normal.

She continued to improve. The conference ended and the university staff moved us into a different dormitory. The dorm mother and several of her staff made gifts for Joanna, including throw pillows and a Care Bear. Finally, after nine days in the hospital, Dr. Kluck said we could return to our home in Wisconsin. We thanked him profusely, but he said, "I didn't do that much. All those prayers were what brought healing."

On the plane going home, I held Joanna on my lap for most of the trip. A mother with a couple of rambunctious children sat in the row ahead of us. When we got off the plane, she turned around and complimented us on how quiet Joanna was. When we told her, "She just spent nine days in the hospital," the mother was silent; I hoped she was giving thanks for her healthy children.

When we arrived home, we made an appointment with a pediatric neurologist in Madison. She told us she could not find any evidence of brain damage from the meningitis and encephalitis. She said Joanna was "lucky," but we knew it wasn't luck; it was the healing hand of God.

Joanna had to learn how to walk again. At first, it was very painful, but in a short time, she was back to normal.

Joanna is now a happy newlywed and enjoying life without any residual effects from her illness. We are confident she made a full recovery because of the grace of God. We praise God for his healing hand on her life.

However, the miracle in my life was that through it all, the Lord gave me "…the peace of God, which transcends all understanding" (Philippians 4:7 NIV).

# Angel in Our Midst

## by Kevin Johnson

Miracles happen and angels do walk amongst us. That is my proclamation and I am blessed and honored to share how both have been a part of my life.

It all started on February 17, 1992. My wife Tracie and I were expecting our first child, and our baby girl came into this world with guns a blazing on that cold winter day in Iowa. Little Miss KayLyn JoAnn Johnson decided not to wait for her due date and joined our family a little over a month early.

This was the early nineties; my cell phone was in a bag in the car. My intentions were to stay close to home as the estimated due date drew closer, but that was still more than a month away. At the time, I was a traveling salesperson and was on the road about five hours away from my wife. I spent the day visiting farms with a veterinarian in eastern Iowa. When I got back to my car, the voice mail on my phone was lit up. Those messages from family members told me I was a father for the first time. However, one message stuck in my mind as I raced across Iowa to get to the hospital. My dad had left a message, "Kevin, you need to get here as soon as possible."

I walked in the hospital room and there they were, my beautiful wife with our new baby girl in her arms—about six hours old. But I sensed something was wrong. It did not take long to realize that something was a little different about KayLyn. She was born with Down syndrome.

Both sets of grandparents were there and they seemed very concerned about the baby, but Tracie and I knew that she was our gift from God. She was beautiful and perfect in our eyes.

As the days progressed, my wife educated herself about Down syndrome, but the more I thought about it, the angrier I became. *Why God? Why did you let this happen to me? Why? I just wanted a normal kid.* Little did I know how this little girl would change my life in so many ways.

Miracle #1: KayLyn taught me how to love. I come from a line of very strong Johnson men. We never shed a tear because that shows weakness. We show no emotion ever and keep it all inside. But as KayLyn grew, my emotions came to the surface. One day just before she started to school, I was in the truck with my best friend when I started crying while sharing my concerns about the possibly of other children making fun of KayLyn at school. Knowing how hurtful children can be to each other, it broke my heart just to think about it. KayLyn changed me that very day and made me a better person.

Miracle #2: We always treated KayLyn the same way we treated her younger siblings. No exceptions; expectations were always high. Her young life touched many people. She has bad days just like everyone else, but she's always ready to give a big hug. She loves Jesus and enjoys singing at church. My wife was the youth minister at our church for four years while Kaylyn was growing up. KayLyn loved the kids and was actively involved in all the activities. At her high school graduation I listened to the seniors talk about how KayLyn, with her hugs and smiles, had been an inspiration to them. Suddenly, it hit home! We truly have an angel in our house every day.

Miracle #3: Moyamoya syndrome on top of Down syndrome, now that is a tough day! Moyamoya is a rare, progressive cerebrovascular disorder caused by blocked arteries at the base of the brain and can be fatal if not treated. We were living in Texas in 2006 and I was hosting a fishing trip for the company I work for, when I got the call to get back to Dallas.

Kaylyn had been losing the use of her leg and her mom had taken her to Dallas to see a specialist. The MRI confirmed she was experiencing multiple mini stokes. More testing showed that the blood supply to one side of her brain had stopped. As we reviewed the MRI, it looked like a rubber band had been applied to the main artery supplying blood to that side of the brain.

Of course, all I wanted to know was how to fix this. A few days later, the doctor removed a section of her skull, took a good artery out and transplanted it to the area of the brain needing blood. They closed the surgery; we prayed diligently as we waited. The surgery was successful. The blood supply started and KayLyn regained the use of her leg. Thanks be to God, there has been no problem with it since! Did I also mention that KayLyn also battled seizures and was on medication from birth to around fourteen years of age, and then one day they just stopped? I call that multiple miracles.

Miracle #4: August 16, 2013, surgeons informed my wife Tracie that she had a tumor the size of a golf ball on her brain stem. I remember the words "life-changing situation" too well. First KayLyn's problems and now Tracie's. The doctors laid out the possibilities: blind, crippled, unable to function normally.

Once again, I asked, "Dear Lord, what do we do now?" Mayo Clinic in Rochester, Minnesota had the answer. On September 9, the surgeon removed a portion of Tracie's skull and carefully chipped away at that tumor. When she awoke, she had no use of the left side of her body. Fourteen days later, she was walking, and we were back in Texas watching our son play varsity football. Would you call that a miracle? I would!

My wife Tracie has always been my strength and the pillar of our family. She believes God gave her that challenge to help her better understand what KayLyn had gone through. It is amazing how the two of them have always connected. As I said before, we are blessed to have an angel living in our home. We know one day God will want her back, but for now, every day is beautiful, and we live joyfully as God allows us to live in her presence. We are abundantly blessed because KayLyn, our angel, is our miracle from God!

# UPDATE:

KayLyn is now 28 years old and living with her Mom and Dad in Elkland, MO. She enjoys Wednesday night Community Ladies Dinners with Mom, Friday lunch dates with Dad and her card ministry. Each week Kaylyn makes her own anniversary, birthday, and get- well cards for friends, family and our church family. KayLyn also stays busy following Dwayne "The Rock" Johnson (favorite actor and boyfriend) and Neal McCoy (favorite singer and boyfriend).

KayLyn now has a niece (Payton Margaret – 2 years old) and enjoys babysitting/ playing and being the "Greatest Aunt Ever." These two have a very special bond and talk everyday via FaceTime. Kaylyn enjoys traveling to Iowa and Texas and spending time with family on a very frequent basis. Our "Angel" continues to bless lives each day with her infectious smile and positive outlook on life.

*Above: KayLyn and The Rock; Below: with Neal McCoy*

# Second Chance at Life

## by Sherry Willetts

On April 2, 2013, Robert and I were visiting our daughter Cortnee in Durham, NC. Robert woke up sick with nausea and dizziness. I thought maybe he had a virus or vertigo, but I soon noticed that his eyes were not focused. I immediately took him to the VA hospital. A team from the ER rushed out to meet us and helped him get inside. Everything was in fast motion. They asked questions and I answered the best I could. They were rushing for tests—all kinds of tests.

Cortnee soon arrived. We waited for answers. If the doctors had any ideas, they did not share them with us. I hoped the neurologist would have an answer, but he didn't.

Suddenly Robert started shaking uncontrollably. It began with his right arm and hand and then his right leg. Next, it moved to his left arm and hand then to his left leg. Then his head began to shake. I attempted to hold him, trying to make the shaking stop, but it continued. This went on for a good while and finally stopped.

He lay motionless, unresponsive. They quickly moved him to the Intensive Care Unit.

Before long a nurse came to the waiting room and said, "Mrs. Willetts, they are taking your husband for another MRI."

When we finally were able to see him again, he was struggling to breathe, and he could not swallow or focus his eyes. The doctors still had no answers. Our other three children were on their way. My head was spinning. I couldn't think straight. The ability to pray eluded me. Cortnee assured me that everything would be okay. "Daddy's a fighter, he's strong and he will be okay. I know he will!" she repeated over and over.

By now, I knew he'd had a stroke, but still no news from the doctors. I stayed by his side all night. The next morning a doctor came in to talk to me.

"Mrs. Willetts, your husband has had a massive stroke to the pons area of the brain stem, the worst possible area of the brain for a stroke. I can't offer you much hope for his recovery. I'm sorry. I need to meet with you and the children to go over the MRI and show you exactly what has happened. Then you'll need to decide what your next step will be."

My worst nightmare had come true. I was at the lowest point of my life. All I could think about was that Robert's life was about to end. I stayed by his side every second, watching him struggle to live.

The doctors and nurses had to suction his throat in order for him to breathe. I couldn't hold back the tears. After a while, he refused to allow them to suction, but I told them to please continue because I knew there was no other option if he was to live.

The only way we could communicate was by his eyes. I would ask questions and he would blink. He was definitely getting worse minute by minute. I tried to pray, but I could not connect with God. I wondered why He felt so far away. It seemed He had deserted me. I asked someone from home to bring my Bible. I knew if I could read God's word, I would feel His presence.

For the next few days, I planned my husband's funeral as I sat by his side. A few weeks ago, we had talked about our wishes when this time came. I thought about all the happy years we had spent together, all the love we had shared. *What would I do without him?*

I'm sure no one is ever prepared for a time like this. Many of our family and friends traveled more than three hours to be with us around the clock. They stayed in the visitor's lounge praying and waiting for news. Churches from all over the country contacted us to say they were praying.

One night a prayer group that our daughter Cortnee meets with came to visit Robert. We gathered around Robert in the ICU unit. We were truly of one accord as we prayed that God would heal Robert if it was His will. The Holy Spirit was definitely present. I finally felt His presence. God *was* there!

The ICU waiting room became a meeting place for family and friends to sit with us, pray with us, and encourage our hearts. We were never alone; the hospital staff could not believe all the support we had. We desperately needed it because the doctors continued to discourage us. They told us repeatedly that there was no hope, that Robert would not survive this, or if he did, he would be in a vegetative state, on life support in a nursing home for the rest of his life. Knowing that "The Lord gives and the Lord takes away" (Job 1:21), we refused to accept that. Robert was in God's hands. It wasn't up to doctors; it was up to God. God had the answer. So we waited for His answer through the long nights and busy days.

Several doctors and nurses prayed with us and this really encouraged us. Our children were such a comfort and stayed by my side as much as they could.

Robert seemed to be declining as his suffering intensified. I remember very clearly the morning that I knew I had to ask him the most important question of all. I was afraid of what his answer would be, but I mustered my strength, leaned over his bed and looked into those brown eyes and asked, "Robert, are you ready to quit fighting?

Immediately his eyes gave me the answer. "No!" I was so happy! Robert and I were ready to fight to the end. From then on, I told the doctors, "Do everything you possibly can to help him recover."

First, the doctors performed a tracheotomy and inserted a feeding tube. Slowly he began to improve. To his delight, they quit suctioning. Some movement came back in his left hand

and he would try to use sign language to communicate. He had learned to sign as a child because he had two cousins who were deaf. I had no clue about sign language, but I made up my mind that I would begin by learning the alphabet. Soon I was spelling out messages to him.

Raw emotion is one of the after effects of a stroke and Robert's emotions were running wild. We would pray and cry—thanking God for all he was doing and all he had done for us.

Doctors were amazed every day at his progress. One day as I sat by his side, I looked up information on my iPad concerning the kind of stroke he'd had. It said the chances of survival was slim. I realized God had given us a miracle. God was going to make Robert better so he could go home. People began to talk about Robert's miracle—and about all the prayers God had answered.

Robert spent four months in the VA hospital and two months in a rest home before coming home. His mind and his memory never faltered. He never missed a beat. He gained strength in all his limbs. His left side is much stronger than his right; we are working on that side. With his iPad, he can read his Bible and study his Sunday school lesson. The VA provided him an electric wheelchair that makes his life much easier. Family and friends helped purchase a piece of exercise equipment that has helped him to move and grow stronger each day. He still can't walk, but he says, "That's okay. I can ride."

On Sunday mornings, Robert rolls into church in his wheelchair and sits right up front. Although his voice is weak, he sings with gusto as he worships the One who gave him life—twice. He gets more hugs every Sunday than anyone else. He continues to be an inspiration to all who know him.

Our life is very different now, but we are learning to adjust. We are blessed! God is good! Our hearts overflow with gratitude for our special miracle—Robert's life.

# A Jolly Miracle

## by Jeanette Levellie

As I dialed my friend Sandra, I tried to calm myself. But it was useless. The minute she answered, my voice cracked along with my heart. "It looks like you'll have only three cats to take care of while we're gone next week. I think we're going to have to put Jolly to sleep."

"Oh, Jeanette, no! What happened?"

Sobs burst from my throat as I paced. "He was acting lethargic last night, he wouldn't eat, and his eyes were dull. I thought I should take him to the vet before we left on our trip, so you didn't have a sick cat on your hands for nine days. The vet said, 'he has a urinary tract infection and a liver problem that requires ten days of antibiotics. But he won't let us near him to give him the meds, so we can't keep him here.' She sounded so grim. When I asked what she'd do in my place, she said she wouldn't keep a cat that she couldn't medicate."

I stopped long enough to wipe the tears dripping off my face. "I can't cancel this speaking trip; I committed to the writers conference director months ago. We leave tomorrow, so it's too late for her to replace me. And I can't ask you to give medicine to Jolly in addition to feeding my three other cats and cleaning their litter boxes for nine days. That's presuming on our friendship."

Sandra's voice was calm and low. "No, no, no, that isn't presuming. I can give Jolly the meds; I've done it with my own cat. How old is he, anyway?"

"Only two—he's my baby. After Angus, my favorite cat ever, disappeared three years ago, I made a vow that I'd never love another cat like I loved him. But I couldn't help myself with this little rascal, Sandra."

I described how Jolly let me carry him around, nuzzling his head against my cheek. He even seemed to relish the goofy baby talk I used for him when I'd hold him up to the mirror and say, "You are such a pretty boy." Before he got sick, I would've been embarrassed to admit that I talked that way to a cat, but now it seemed not so silly after all.

"Well, we're not going to give up on him that easy, Jeanette. I'll come over tonight and you can show me what to do, okay?"

I released a grateful, ragged sigh. "Okay—see you tonight. And thanks—you're a jewel."

When I came through the door from work, my only greeting for my husband Kevin was, "Where's Jolly?"

"I'm not sure, Jeanette. We had a horrible time transferring him from the cage at the vet's into the carrier—he growled, clawed, and hissed at me. Even the vet's assistant was afraid of him."

I argued as I hunted for my fur baby. "He was scared, Kev. If a stranger stuck needles in you, then put you in a cage overnight, you'd be none too thrilled with them either. Oh, here he is."

Jolly lay curled in a fetal position on the floor of my closet, his eyes turned down at the corners. He was too weak to cry, but when he saw me kneel down beside him, he started purring.

"Oh, Jolly," I moaned, "I'm so sorry you're sick. Please don't die, okay? I love you so much. Please get well." I alternated between begging Jolly to recover and asking God to heal him while I stroked his head and back. When Sandra rang the doorbell twenty minutes later, I was lying on the carpet next to Jolly, all thoughts of dinner and my upcoming trip erased from my mind.

While Sandra asked about the trip, I managed to squirt a syringe-full of medicine into the side of Jolly's mouth. The whole time he swallowed it, he growled at me. "I'm sorry, Baby," I crooned, "but this nasty-tasting stuff will make you better." He soon drifted off to sleep. I woke up a dozen times that night, hoping I'd find him still alive in the morning.

When I peeked into the closet at daybreak the next morning, Jolly was gone. That gave me a slice of hope. At least he could walk.

After I found him, I tried to give him another dose of medicine before leaving town. He growled and spit it out. "I hope we're doing the right thing by leaving him," I whimpered to Kevin. "What if he won't let Sandra give him any meds?"

Kevin hugged me for a long time. "I think he'll be okay, Jeanette. Between Sandra and God, he's in good hands." I squeezed my eyes shut to keep the tears from dripping out.

We'd barely left the driveway when I texted Sandra. "No meds down Jolly. Hope u can manage it 2nite. Thx again!"

I tried not to fret while traveling through the gorgeous Ohio and Pennsylvania highways and speaking to aspiring writers over the next nine days. Sandra's texts to me didn't help much. "Jolly purrs when I feed him, but growls when med dropper appears. Sorry!"

Forcing myself to push aside mental images of returning home to a kitty funeral, I repeatedly prayed the only thoughts I could muster, "Please heal my baby, Lord."

As we pulled into the driveway, I asked Kevin to let me out before he drove into the garage. "I have to see Jolly," I cried.

When he heard my voice, Jolly came running from the den to greet me, purring loudly and rubbing against my ankles. I scooped him into my arms and sunk my face into his neck. "How have you been, buddy? Did you miss me?" I glanced at the bottle of mustard-colored liquid sitting on the kitchen counter—almost full, just like it was nine days ago. I sighed.

"Let's try this," I said, squirting some medicine into a spoonful of wet food. He lapped it up like it was beef stroganoff. "Honey, come see this!" I hollered to Kevin.

Kev stopped unpacking the car long enough to pop into the kitchen.

"Jolly is eating this medicine in food. Why didn't I think of this before? Sandra's been trying to get it down him this whole time by squirting the syringe in his mouth."

"But Jeanette," Kevin said, "I wonder if he doesn't need the medicine now. He looks as healthy as ever."

I took a serious look at Jolly then, standing on his hind legs, scratching at the back door to go out, catch a mouse, and bring it to me as a welcome home gift. When I opened the door, he bounded onto the lawn.

I chuckled. "You're right—he is back to normal. But I'll give him the meds till they're done anyway, since I paid so much for them."

I know that God often uses vets to heal our beloved animals. But this time, He reached down in pity toward my aching heart while a bottle of medicine sat on the counter, untouched. As I watched my fur baby skitter across the lawn like a shooting star going sideways, I wiped the happy tears away, thankful for our Jolly miracle.

# Light a Candle

## by J. Martin

An old proverb says, "It is better to light a candle than to curse the darkness." One sad day I found this so true. So very true.

Some say my daughter was trying to commit suicide when she rammed her car into that huge tree in the farmer's yard. Her little son was killed and she suffered a life-threatening and life-changing traumatic brain injury.

But she lived. I knew my life and hers were changed forever by this event. At first, I did not light candles.

I wasn't prepared for what was to come. Is a parent ever prepared to learn a beloved child struggles with addictions? Shock and disbelief hung on my every waking moment, until my strong faith in God propelled me to action. Slow action, I must say, because after 25 years in health care, I cringed just to think of what lay ahead. I knew something about the struggles of a traumatic-brain-injury patient.

The daughter we knew was gone. A new daughter lay unconscious, only into the first year of her second marriage.

First, pressing upon us, much like all the foreign tubes and machines pressing upon our daughter's young body was the need to bury our grandson. Some lives on this earth are short; only six years old, he held the proud title of first grandson. We laid him to rest in a small, country cemetery surrounded by beautiful trees and lush greenery.

After the funeral, still dazed, I returned to the Intensive Care Unit. I worried grief would take our daughter down if we told her about her son's death, but God, in His mercy, shielded her brain and emotions. She didn't have a clue about what had happened for a very long time. She was barely alive.

Her husband was supportive, but we differed on various aspects of her medical care and dialogue wasn't easy. Since he was her husband, I had no say and I never felt so helpless in my life. We didn't relate well at all; perhaps, because I felt he was partially responsible for where she was.

This was a dark journey. I barely crawled to God. I shoved my anger at Him. I lashed out.

I felt so alone. I pleaded. *Why? Why, God? Had I not lived a Christian life?* Even my dear husband handled his grief differently than I and we were often in conflict.

I was a mother bereft. During my initial grief, God sent me two ministering angels. To this day, I can still tell you the color of his eyes and see those freckles on her face. This gift of angels was a miracle for me just when I needed it most.

The alcohol and drug charges, culminating in the unlawful death of our grandson, eventually sent our thirty-two-year old daughter to prison. Although I did grieve for my now former son-in-law because he had lost his first-born son, I partially blamed him for what happened.

My lawyer, however, said there was no way, in our county, that in her condition she would have been sent to prison. But in the county where the accident happened, she was.

Thus began a darker chapter for us. I had trouble believing the whole chain of events. My twelve-year-old granddaughter went to live with her father, five hours away. My heart stung with another loss. We filed for grandparents' rights. When our granddaughter later visited, we had to make sure she saw her mother, even if it meant seeing her behind bars.

The ensuing months and years were not easy. I spent many sleepless nights. I wrestled with God, who had always been the stronghold in my life. Since I had learned long ago to lean on Him, I clung to Him. I fled to His word. I embraced the essence of the old prophet Habukkah, who said, "Though the fig tree does not bud and there are no grapes on the vine … yet will I rejoice in the Lord." (Hab 3 17-19)

With the passing of time and much prayer and faith, I quit asking God "Why?" and simply trusted Him. I knew that bad things do sometimes happen to good people. This was just part of life. I knew that God was on every journey with me, even when I didn't feel His presence, He was there.

I welcomed God's sovereignty in my life and I knew the sweetness of living in His love and care. Our family survived.

Not only survived, but after the roller coaster of sadness and prolonged grief, God blessed us beyond belief. He always knew what was best for us.

Our daughter was released from prison early for good behavior; her husband hung in there with her for several years afterwards. Our granddaughter has done well and has been blessed in so many ways.

Most importantly, our daughter recovered in an incredible way, one which I consider a miracle in itself. Given her injuries, she should have died in the accident, but she didn't. Hers was a slow and arduous recovery which included learning to crawl, walk, talk and write again. I have seen her climb heights I never dreamed were possible. It's true, she is not the same daughter we knew, but she is still our daughter and we have learned to love her for who she is today.

Her very life is a miracle and I know God is not finished with her yet. She lives alone now, happy and safe. She brings joy to our lives, and she has a great relationship with her daughter. We celebrate her little son's life each anniversary. Her faith and Christian walk astound me. God uses her in ministry in so many ways.

A few years into her recovery process, I knew writing our story would help us heal, but my daughter wasn't ready to face her story in print. She was still crushed and ashamed. Then, a year later, she called. "Mom, I want to tell my story so that others will not go through the same thing."

Oh, how I had prayed for that.

So, we wrote her story. God gave us a publisher and success with sales. That was several years ago, but tragedy is universal and grief is evergreen. So the story goes on—and on.

Our story is not unique; it is just our story. We want God to be glorified and we want people to know miracles take many forms. When they happen, you know it in your heart.

# A Flight to Remember

### by Maggie Matthews

My husband and I were taking four-month-old Katie home to see her grandparents. They were overwhelmed with joy at the prospect of seeing her for the first time. Meeting Katie would bring many surprises. She was a bundle of energy, a real charmer, and had the most beautiful blue eyes in the world. When we made her picture, the first thing you'd notice were her eyes.

We were so excited as we headed for the airport. Jim carried the luggage and I carried the baby in her seat. It was a small airport, and most of the passengers were military personnel going home on leave. Everyone chatted excitedly, talking about how great it would be to see family and friends at home and to eat Mom's cooking.

After what seemed endless hours, the plane was ready and we boarded. I fastened the infant seat and sat down near the window, leaving the aisle seat for Jim. *Oh God, thank you so much for making this trip possible. I can't wait to see Mama and for her to see Katie.*

The plane was loaded to capacity. The attendant's voice came over the intercom with the usual "Fasten your seat belts and extinguish all smoking material."

Finally, we took off. I closed my eyes and imagined what it would be like to watch my mother hold my baby girl for the first time. I had missed my mother so much since we went to Europe a year ago. I understood what the Psalmist meant when he said: "… my cup runneth over." I was happier than I had ever been in my life. I breathed a prayer, *Thank you, God.*

Jim was talking to the Air Force sergeant across the aisle while I was lost in my own little world. Katie was sleeping peacefully, looking like an angel.

Suddenly there was a lot of chatter and everyone was looking and pointing down the aisle toward the back of the plane. I raised up in my seat and looked to see what was happening.

A reddish fluid was running down the passenger aisle. The look on Jim's face told me he was afraid although I knew he would never admit it. *What was it?* There was a clamor on the plane, bordering on panic. An airman who was an airplane mechanic said it was hydraulic fluid.

Now I was afraid! Were we going to die? *Please, God, don't let us die. What about the baby you gave us? And what about Mama? She's just getting over Daddy's death. Please, God, calm my spirit. "When I am afraid I will trust in you." Help me to trust in you. Give me your peace.*

The memories are as vivid as if it happened yesterday—
the smell of the hydraulic fluid, the fear on everyone's face.
The tears were just below the surface; I choked to hold them
back.

Jim smiled at me and offered his hand to comfort me.
"Honey, if it were anything serious, we'd turn around and go
back. I'm sure there's a backup system for whatever is wrong.
Don't worry now. I'm sure everything's going to be all right."

I wasn't so sure. We were 10,000 feet above the earth and
something was leaking hydraulic fluid. I closed my eyes again
to hide the tears; I didn't want him to see how scared I was.

Katie woke up and started to cry. It was time for her to
eat. At least I had something else to think about for a few
minutes. I pulled her bottle from the bag and gave it to her. Her
blue eyes searched the plane, all new and strange to her. Her
gaze came to rest upon her daddy's face and she broke into a
big smile; she was a daddy's girl.

*What was going on? Why didn't the pilot do something?*
*Why didn't he let us know what was happening? Well, if we*
*were going to die, it would be together—the man I loved and*
*our baby. Please, God, please take care of us.*

The pilot came over the intercom with a message: "Fasten
your seatbelts and extinguish all smoking materials. There is a
mechanical problem and we have been redirected to Frankfurt
airport."

I wondered how long it would be. It couldn't be very long. I looked at my watch and noted that we had only been in the air twenty-five minutes. *But how much hydraulic fluid was left? Will there be enough to get us back to the airport and a safe landing?*

I couldn't help watching the time, counting the minutes. It had been twenty minutes since we turned around. Katie was asleep again. Jim held my hand tightly. One lady was throwing up from the stench of the fluid or perhaps from fear. The crew was trying to console everyone and assure us that everything was under control.

As we began our descent, the plane started to shake violently. The shaking of the plane woke the baby and she began to cry. I wanted to take her out of the seat and hold her, but I was afraid.

The pilot's voice again. "Fasten your seatbelts. We will be landing momentarily. If you look out the window, you can see the airport to our right. When the plane lands, please remain seated. You will be instructed about how to disembark and board another aircraft. I will not be your pilot on that plane. Have a good trip home."

A few seconds later, we landed with a big bump on the tarmac. The landing gear had worked! Now that we were safely on the ground again, emotions ruled. We were hysterically happy. There was a lot of back-slapping and hugging. Some laughed and a few cried. *Surely none of us would ever be the same.* A brush with death had taught us how fragile life is. From now on, I would cherish each day and count every blessing.

I felt like singing "How Great Thou Art." Instead, I prayed. *Thank you, God, for being with us, for keeping us safe. I felt as if my heart would burst with gratitude.*

We had witnessed a miracle. We could have died that day, but God kept us safe. I remembered Deuteronomy 33:27, "The eternal God is our refuge and underneath are the everlasting arms." *Mama used to quote that verse all the time. My husband, my baby, and I were going home. Day after tomorrow Katie would meet her grandparents.*

# UPDATE:

*Katie* is thirty now and has a little girl of her own. After four years in the U. S. Air Force, she returned to North Carolina, but continues service in the Air Force Reserve. She completed her college degree and is employed as a science teacher in public school. Her only child is in first grade and the center of her world.

# A Gift of Life

## by Martha Pittman Hales

My husband Eb and I married in 1972 and moved to Wilmington, NC. We joined Murray Memorial Baptist Church, and our pastor, Reverend B. A. Porter and his wife Peg became our parents away from home. I know now that God was putting us with people who would help us through a very difficult time in our lives.

Some months prior to our son Alex's birth, our church nominating committee asked me to be WMU (Woman's Missionary Union) director. My mother had been part of the WMU, but I was only twenty-four and had no idea what the job involved. I attended a leader's conference, where I met the WMU director for the Wilmington Baptist Association, a dynamic Christian named Norma. She offered to help me with WMU and invited me to her home. During my visit, I learned that she had a son with Down syndrome. Not long after that I found out I was pregnant, but never expected that my baby would have the same problem.

When we received news that our baby had Down syndrome, I called Norma because I knew she would understand my feelings.

On April 4, 1975, our first child, Alex, was born and the next year the doctors told us he needed open-heart surgery. Our pediatrician, Dr. George Koseruba, made an appointment for Alex to see a cardiologist from Chapel Hill. They performed a heart catheterization and found a large hole in Alex's heart, partly in both chambers. Surgery would be risky, but without it, Alex's life would be cut short.

The doctors were not very encouraging. They said that some parents of a child with this type of disability opted not to have the surgery since the child would never be "normal." Eb and I told the doctors that we wanted to give Alex the opportunity to have a good life and we wanted to go ahead with surgery. The doctors said his chances of surviving the operation were less than fifty-fifty.

We were surrounded by love, everyone praying for us—our family and friends, Mr. Porter and Peg, our church family. And especially Norma, who understood me. Surely God placed her in my life at this time for a purpose. He used her to offer practical help, inspiration, and encouragement.

On April 4, 1976, Alex celebrated his first birthday. The doctor scheduled his surgery for August. I was teaching in an elementary school, and worked with three teachers who were devout Christians. They met in one of the classrooms after school to pray. When I told them about Alex's upcoming surgery, they invited me to join them. God had added three more prayer warriors to Alex's team. I remember one of them,

Margaret, quoted Matthew 18:19 "Again I say unto you, that if two of you shall agree on earth as touching anything that they shall ask, it shall be done for them of my Father which is in heaven." We prayed that the surgery would be successful and for the Lord to heal Alex. Diana, another teacher, said "Sometimes God heals by taking people to be with Him," but she believed that Alex would live. I wanted to believe that too, but it was hard not to be anxious.

I continued my work with WMU, and at another meeting, I sat beside a lady who introduced herself as Dorothy Moore. She became another prayer warrior and a lifelong friend.

Many of the WMU directors from other churches put Alex on their prayer lists. Our church family was praying, as well as our home churches.

As August drew near, I had to decide if I would take a leave of absence or quit my teaching job. Eb and I decided that if Alex didn't survive the surgery, I would return to school, but if he lived, I would resign and be a stay-at-home Mom.

When the time came, we anxiously traveled to Chapel Hill. Mr. and Mrs. Porter were there that day. Mr. Porter prayed for Alex and we waited. While in the surgical waiting area, I received a telegram from a woman in my home church in Broadway, NC. She was a dear family friend and childhood Sunday school teacher. The telegram simply said, "With you by way of prayer." At the WMU convention in Ridgecrest, NC, all the women were praying. People were praying everywhere!

When the surgeon came out, he told us that they had used two patches to close the hole in both heart chambers. The next few days would be critical.

The second night after surgery, we received a call from the hospital—Alex was in serious trouble. His kidneys were not functioning, and his body was filling with fluid, causing pressure on his brain. He had a seizure; his heart stopped; and he stopped breathing. He was placed on life support.

It was around two a.m., but Eb told me to call Mr. Porter and ask him to start a prayer chain. The doctors said that they did not think Alex would live through the next hour.

All night I agonized in prayer, asking God to give Alex back the breath of life. As daylight came, he was still holding on to life. One of the nurses came out, and I asked if Alex had breathed any on his own. When she said "Yes," the doctors shook their heads and said, "We didn't do it." I believed that was my sign from God that Alex would live.

For a few days, he seemed to improve, but then the patch in his heart started breaking up his red blood cells with every heartbeat. He needed blood transfusions to stay alive. Still people were praying and believing. James 5:14-16a says, "Is any sick among you? Let him call for the elders of the church: and let them pray over him, anointing him with oil in the name of the Lord; and the prayer of faith shall save the sick, and the Lord shall raise him up."

Eb's mother, Aunt Hettie, and his sister Dorothy came to visit. Aunt Hettie had a little bottle of oil from the Holy Land and she went in to Alex and anointed him with the oil, "I know he will be healed," she said. We also had a visit from our friends, David and Patsy Williamson. As we talked about Alex's condition, David quoted James 5:16b, "the effectual fervent prayer of a righteous man availeth much" (KJV). I am sure that David had faith in the healing power of prayer.

One day in our room, I got on my knees before the Lord, confused about how to pray.

I wanted Alex to live, but I didn't know if it was God's will. I knew there was a Scripture about the Holy Spirit interceding when we didn't know how to pray. "Likewise, the Spirit also helpeth our infirmities: for we know not what we should pray for as we ought: but the Spirit itself maketh intercession for us with groanings which cannot be uttered. And he that searcheth the hearts knoweth what is the mind of the Spirit, because he maketh intercession for the saints according to the will of God" (Romans 8:26-27 KJV). I finally gave it all to God.

We had been in Chapel Hill for a month when we finally got some good news. Alex's own tissue was growing into the patch in his heart! The red blood cells had stopped breaking up. God had heard every prayer. We had a miracle! We were going home!

I believe that God worked through the faith and prayers of many people to bring about this miracle of healing. Looking back at events that occurred, I can see how God placed certain people in my life to help me through a season of growing through my trials.

I promised God that I would give Him the glory if Alex lived. I will never stop praising Him for placing this special, loving child in our care thirty-nine years ago, and for all the lessons of life and love He has taught us through Alex.

# The Day the Brick Wall Fell

## by Joy E. Miller

"You know when I sit and when I rise; you perceive my thoughts from afar. You discern my going out and my lying down; you are familiar with all my ways." (Ps. 139:2-3 NIV)

I felt invisible and alone at this point. I was in my early twenties, and I still lived at home with my parents. Another friend had recently gotten engaged. I was doing a monotonous data entry job that was far from fulfilling. Every day I went to work wondering if God was even aware of me and my unmet desires.

One morning I drove to the small corporate office where I worked. Turning into the parking lot, I was grateful to get a spot close to the street. I pulled in, parking in front of an abandoned downtown brick building. A few minutes later, coffee in hand, I settled into my chair in my windowless office. As usual, I had brought my lunch, but at the last minute, I decided I needed some sunshine so I went out for my meal. I rarely gave myself this luxury, but I wanted a break from my computer. When I returned, the parking lot was full. My prime space was taken, and I had to park on the opposite side of the lot.

After work, I hurried to my car, on the way to meet a friend, passing my former parking place. I got in, put the car in reverse and started to back out. Suddenly I heard a horrible crash. *What was happening? What was that loud noise?* In disbelief, I watched in my rearview mirror as the façade of the ancient brick building tumbled down in one motion. Bricks pelted the row of cars parked beneath ... including the car that had taken my space. It happened so fast. I could not believe that, where a few moments ago there had been a wall, now there was a pile of debris laying on numerous vehicles and the nearby sidewalk. "Jesus," I said. "Thank you, Jesus!" If I had left one minute later, I could have been seriously injured or killed. I called one of my co-workers and told her what had just transpired. I told her to alert the other employees to the damage.

I slowly pulled away as curious onlookers started approaching. Wow! God did see me. He had not forgotten me. He saw exactly where I was and what I was doing. Not only that but He cared about my well-being. I felt a huge wave of warmth and amazement wash over me.

That morning I didn't feel God's presence, but He was faithfully orchestrating each moment of my day. He prompted me to leave for lunch and because of that, I was kept safe. He even kept my car from being destroyed. My circumstances hadn't changed in those few hours. I was still single and still in a job I didn't enjoy, but those facts didn't overwhelm me anymore. God's miraculous intervention to protect me from the brick wall renewed my faith in His love for me. He was actively working in my life, and He had everything under control.

The Psalmist says God is familiar with all our ways. He knows us by name. We may feel lost in the crowd at times but He knows our thoughts, our concerns, and our struggles. Scripture shows us time and again, how God worked in individuals' lives in an intimate way.

God is fashioning my story and often it doesn't go in the direction I expect it to go. I've been hurt by unfulfilled dreams. Now when I am disheartened, I take time to put my thoughts and feelings down on paper. I also make note of my prayer requests, questions, and God's blessings. I can look back at my journal and see God's handiwork in my life.

When I am discouraged, I find comfort in reading the Psalms—David's journal— and by reviewing my own "passage markers" to recall how God has been faithful to me in the most painful of times. He is Immanuel, God with us. He sees every tear and listens to every question. His plans for me are very specific and special. It's incredible to see the miracles, big and small, that God orchestrates in each life.

# Update

Many years have passed since that brick wall fell. Various jobs as well as a twenty-year battle with depression have taught me that I need a fresh supply of God's love, wisdom, and courage every day.

At one job my boss couldn't handle stress, so she passed it on to those around her. I dreaded going in each day. One morning as I walked to my office, I prayed for help. Something at the edge of the sidewalk caught my eye. It was a beautifully painted rock. I picked it up, studying the butterfly with bright, green and pink wings against an iridescent blue background.

Butterflies signify life to me. I held it tight. I knew God was saying, "I see you, Joy. I am with you. You are not alone." Once again God had given me a sign that He sees me and will take care of me.

# *Found*

## by Ane Mulligan

On a hot July morning, sipping a cup of coffee, I opened my e-mail. Nothing breath-taking about that, except on this particular day, I was asked a question that irrevocably changed my life.

"Are you the Ane Mulligan looking for your birth mother, Elsie Vauna Mullvain?"

I'd always known I was adopted, and my childhood was idyllic. I was a child of the fifties, when Cokes were a nickel and roller skates had keys. The only thing that ever bothered me was I didn't look like anybody. That started me wondering.

I became a people watcher. Was that woman my mom? Could that man be my dad? Did I have any sisters? One time, I must have been about ten, I followed a woman up and down the aisles in the grocery store. She finally asked me if I was lost. My mom found me about that time, apologized to the woman, and thoroughly embarrassed, took me home. It didn't matter. Up close, that woman didn't look as much like me as I first thought.

I was disappointed but not daunted. I continued to stare in the mirror, searching my own face for someone. After I married and had a child, I finally had someone who looked like me. I put away my longing.

In 1998, I got a letter from my dad. It wasn't his favored yellow legal paper. It the kind of blue stock they use for official court documents. Premonition made my heart pound. I slid it from its envelope.

### The adoption of Roberta Ann Mullvain

Suddenly I wasn't me anymore. But who was I? I opened it and scanned its pages, until I saw my mother's name. Elsie V. Mullvain.

A myriad of emotions whirled. Scenarios played out and were cast aside. Tears of joy welled as I thought of open arms welcoming me, then quickly turned to sorrow with the fear of rejection. I tried to picture her, but her face remained shadowed.

For a writer, I was an empty page. I didn't know what I wanted to do, so I put my adoption papers in the safe and closed the door. After a few months, curiosity won out. I posted my mother's and my name on an adoption search board. I also sent out some letters to all the Mullvains. I received quite a few answers from distant and not-so-distant cousins.

From one, I learned I had sisters! Growing up, I had a loving relationship with my adopted brother, but I'd always wanted a sister and now had three … somewhere. Then I found Elsie. I received a letter from her with a little information, only she didn't want a relationship. I was sorry, but I honored her request. I did send flowers for her birthday that year with a note that said, "Thank you. Love, Ane." I wanted her to know I understood.

But I prayed and hoped that somehow, maybe one day I could find my sisters. Once again, my overactive imagination kicked into high gear. Would they want to know me? Were they like me?

Maybe after my mother passed away, I could search. I only had one problem. I didn't know their names. It would be difficult to search without those—not only that, they were most likely married with new names. And if I managed to find them, how would I approach them? Reluctantly, I put the dream into God's hands. It was never out of my heart, though.

On June 10th, 2001, my adopted mother went to be with the Lord. Three months later, Dad joined her. I felt like I was truly an orphan, and I began to think more and more about my sisters. Two years later, a woman at my church, knowing I was adopted, excitedly told me she and her husband were adopting a baby. I thought, "What if that baby was the grandchild of one of my sisters?"

From that "what if," I wrote a novel, and Elsie's story was part of the inspiration for the manuscript. For my next book, I wrote one that chronicled a young woman's search of for her birthmother. By then, I'd written all I knew on the adoption theme, and the story was ended. Had mine ended as well?

God has His own timing and a delightful sense of surprise.
On July 18th, 2009, ten long years after I posted on that
adoption board, I got that life-changing e-mail from a woman
named Linda, asking the breath-taking question: Are you the
Ane Mulligan looking for your birthmother, Elsie Vauna
Mullvain?

After confirming I was, she proceeded to tell me my
mother died in 2007. She also told me I had 5 sisters. Five? I
felt like I'd won the Publisher's Clearinghouse Sweepstakes!

Then she sent me a copy of my mother's obituary from the
newspaper, which included a photo. It was like a mirror. For
the first time in my life, I looked like someone. I felt like I'd
come home from a long journey. For me, the bond was instant.
I "knew" what she'd gone through. I understood the betrayal
she'd experienced. The heartbreak. And I knew she'd loved
me.

The next e-mail brought a photo of my sister Pam. She
had my face, too! One of my friends photoshopped my red hair
onto my sister and we became twins, although she's almost
eight years younger than me.

Linda had handed me the greatest gift I'd ever received.
But she had a gift-topper. She sent a link for Elsie's online
memorial. There, I saw all my sisters and Elsie's pictorial life. I
couldn't believe the resemblance. There were childhood photos
of my mother that were identical to mine, reflecting who I was
and everything I knew about myself. I saw her laughing, head

tossed back, and captured her personality. And she was identical to me.

I wanted so badly to meet my sisters, but I left it to Linda and her sister, Yvonne (who babysat my sisters when they were young). I didn't want to tarnish my sisters' memory of our mother, nor did I want to disrupt their lives.

I will be forever indebted to Linda and Yvonne. They decided they'd want to know if the roles were reversed. Yvonne called my sister Trish. Within minutes of that phone call, I received an e-mail. The subject line read: Hi, Big Sister!

After several e-mails, filled with details about the family, I called Trish. The sound of her voice as she answered the phone with, "Hey, big sis," filled my eyes with tears and lodged a lump in my throat the size of Texas. Together we laughed and talked for more than 90 minutes. Her personality was so much like mine I could hardly believe it.

On the Friday before Halloween, I flew to Seattle, where they all live. They met me at the airport, and we hugged, cried, and laughed. The first thing baby sister Cindy (how I love saying that!) did was to grab my hands and examine them. Her ocean-wide smile and nod told me I had her hands. Mullvain hands. Now, I understand the old saying that blood is thicker than water.

They opened their arms and their lives to me. It was beyond amazing. There was no need to get to know one another. We're so much alike all we had to do was catch up on our lives. Things I'd always thought were due to my upbringing and environment (like my love of books and even mannerisms) turned out to be in my DNA. Who knew?

On Sunday, my sister Debby Jo threw a family reunion for me to meet my brothers-in-law, my nieces and nephews. They also invited their late dad's sisters. When I walked in the door, their Aunt Andy stared at me, agape.

"If I didn't know better," Andy said, "I'd swear I was seeing a ghost. You're a clone of your mother. In fact, of all you girls, you look the most like Elsie."

What a beautiful gift!

The emotions of finding and connecting with my sisters still bring tears to my eyes. Tears of gratitude. To God, my Savior, for keeping my dream safe in His heart to be fulfilled in His time. And to Linda and Yvonne for obeying the nudge God gave them to contact me. And to my sisters for opening their lives and hearts to me.

Debby Jo said it best. She told me when I came through her door and she saw me, her first thought was, "She's finally come home."

She was right. I'd spent a lifetime lost, and now I'm found.

Another version of this story is under consideration at Munce Group Magazine.

# My Son, My Amazing Miracle

by Trish Nixon

The last answer was given that Sunday morning in our women's Sunday school class. The question was, "Could you find it in your heart to endure a trial a second time if you knew it was God's will and purpose for you?"

Our radiant-faced teacher was about to continue when I whispered a barely audible, "No." The room of nearly forty women grew silent as each sat waiting for an explanation. "I'm pregnant," I whispered. The women in the room knew my story. They understood.

A few years earlier, I had spoken at a Mother's Day brunch before 150 women. I had shared my hope and prayer that each of them would come to know the Holy Spirit in the fullness of His ministry as comforter and guide as I had. I described to them how, six weeks after I miscarried, I sat in the living room alone crying. My two daughters were already tucked into bed and their father was working a late shift when the reality hit me that I was no longer pregnant. I tried to reason that there were twins and one was taken and I was still carrying the other. After all, my body and hormones seemed to be telling me I was still pregnant. However, my mind really did know the truth; I just did not want to accept it.

As I cried, I was suddenly aware of a presence in the room. I looked up hoping it was not one of my daughters. I did not want them to see me in that state. Instantly, I knew it was the Holy Spirit and He was crying with me. When I asked Him why, His simple reply was, "I came to share your grief." With that, I really lost it. To this day, I am not sure if I was crying harder because of the pain of losing my baby, or because I was so touched by God's faithfulness and compassion. The reality of the millions of people in the world, many of them grieving about some tragedy in their lives, and yet He was there with *me*. I was so honored, so humbled.

I began to pour out all of my hurts, telling Him I was so afraid that He was going to start with my baby and then take my girls away from me. After you have experienced loss, your fear is that you will lose even more. I could not bear the thought of losing my girls, and yet my mind was becoming consumed with "vain imaginations" and horrors. To which He very softly said, "Give us this day our daily bread."

"What in the world does daily bread have to do with my daughters?" I questioned, admittedly a tad annoyed.

His reply was so profound I still feel … overwhelmed with relief, comforted, and, well, I just can't put it all into words. "You are horrified about an event that has not occurred. If and when I choose to take your daughters home, I will give you the grace you need to handle it. Right now, you are all worked up about something that has not happened."

Honestly, I cannot remember if I even responded. He showed me all of the near death calls we had experienced and how He had protected us. He assured me He had plans for my daughters' lives. He then showed me my precious baby in the protecting arms of Father God.

I was at peace until nine months later when my gynecologist said, "It looks like what happened several months ago may happen with this baby too." My world spun out of control as I faced another miscarriage. I was mad and confused. Our marriage was not going that well. Was this God's way of saying, "You don't need any more children"? There was a forbearing sense of hopelessness. Of course, the Holy Spirit was faithful to come and share my brokenness. In fact, three times that very day He tried to come and minister to me, but I told Him to go away. I was too hurt and angry.

I remained committed to my leadership positions, giving words of knowledge and comfort to others, but I would not let Him minister to me. Because He does not infringe upon our free will, He waited until I was ready. Several friends were having babies; one in particular needed baby clothes. She was expecting her sixth child. Slowly, I climbed the attic stairs to do the right thing, sow into another's need. As I unwrapped clothes and placed them in a box, in a way, the box became a coffin. I was putting my dreams, my hopes, and my aching heart into the box. I began to weep and He was immediately there. Oh, the faithfulness of our God.

The weeks turned into months. Those friends had their babies. I even gave one of them a shower. Life would go on and it was up to me how I would handle it. Was I going to be an example to my daughters and those to whom I ministered about trusting God even in the midst of heartache and pain? Or would I allow Satan free reign of my soul? Although I chose to trust God, it was a healing process.

And that Sunday morning was part of the process. In my humanness I had to admit that even though I trusted God, I could not trust my emotions if the precious life that was growing within me ended in another home-going.

My honest reply of "No" not only opened the door for me to receive prayer and encouragement, it opened the door for others to be real and honest about their feelings and trials. Those dear sisters in Christ stood with me in prayer for the safety and health of the new baby— not only that morning, but also for the remaining months of my pregnancy. It was not easy for the radiant-faced teacher. She had lost a child and knew exactly what I was going through. Rather than run from my pain, she was able to walk along beside me and share it. She too had to allow God to heal her broken heart.

Near the end of the pregnancy, complications arose and there was great physical pain. I cried out and assured God this was one time He had no clue about what I was feeling, after all

He was a man. Several days after my uncontrolled outburst, He again appeared to me. Gently, He said, "I just wanted you to know I do understand your pain."

Now I was really feeling ashamed. I felt the warmth of His smile as if He were saying, "That's a woman for you." Then, gently, He responded with, "Remember the cross. I gave my only Son for you."

Indeed, He understood not only the physical and emotional pain, He also understood the pain of losing His only Son. I have the peaceful assurance of knowing where my babies are. He, tragically, has the harsh reality that many reject His Son.

In the early days of my pregnancy, God led me to Psalms 126:5-6, "Those who sow in tears shall reap in joy. He who continually goes forth weeping, bearing seed for sowing, shall doubtless come again with rejoicing, bringing his sheaves *with him.*" (NKJV)

That pregnancy ended with the birth of my son twenty years ago. Today he serves as a constant reminder of God's understanding and faithfulness. After much suffering, God truly gave me an amazing miracle.

# God Is Doing a New Thing

## by Julie Pickern

My life had been happy and fulfilling. I met the love of my life when we were in college. We shared the same dream of one day becoming missionaries. Soon after college, we were married. Gene entered the ministry and became a successful pastor. We had two beautiful children, a boy and a girl. I could not have been happier.

Then in 2001, our dream came true—we were appointed missionaries to Dominican Republic. We spent the next nine years learning how to be missionaries—building relationships, sharing God's love with the people, teaching them the Bible, and ministering to physical needs. Those were wonderful, productive years.

But in June 2010, I became very ill. At first, they thought I'd had a stroke. I got progressively worse, and a few days later, I could not walk. The International Mission Board decided to send me home to Pensacola, Florida for treatment. En route to Pensacola, we stopped in Atlanta and by that time, I was too weak to stand up. The nurse traveling with me recommended that they call an ambulance and take me to the hospital in Atlanta.

There the doctors discovered a mass on my brain stem. Although they never told me, they told my family that I might only live two weeks. I vaguely remember amidst the fog, seeing family members coming in and out of the room.

Because I was a missionary, the International Mission Board notified missionaries around the world of my illness and asked them and their people group to pray for me. It stirs my heart to think of people talking to God about me in many different languages. God heard their prayers and raised me up. After several days, I was well enough to travel by ambulance to Pensacola where I received excellent care. I was in the hospital for a long time and underwent many tests. My final diagnosis was Multiple Sclerosis. I went from the hospital to the nursing home with little hope of ever leaving there.

This was one of the hardest things I have ever faced. I was not afraid to die; I knew where I was going. But this? I was too young to be in a nursing home. I turned fifty while I was there. The doctors weren't sure I'd live to see my next birthday or the next one.

I was in a wheelchair, but did not have the strength to move it. I tried to lift the left hand brake on my chair, but I couldn't; I thought the brake was broken. I got in another wheelchair, and that left brake would not work, then another chair. Finally, I realized that it was my left side that had been affected by the stroke. The wheel chair was not defective; I was!

I had to depend on someone to help me do everything—eat, dress, bathe. However, I had the absolute best care possible. My nurses and nursing assistants were wonderful. They tried to find time to talk with me and the other patients, but most of all they prayed with us.

Just before I left the Dominican Republic, I had been studying the book of Isaiah, so I continued. Because of MS, my vision was blurred and reading was extremely difficult. I started reading Isaiah 43. It began, "God is doing a new thing, Can you see it?" I couldn't see it clearly, so I blinked and tried again—three times I tried to see it, and then, BAM! It was as clear as a bell. *God is doing a new thing. Can you see it?* And I said out loud, "Yes Lord, I see it!"

Knowing He was going to begin something new in my life brought perfect peace. I continued to read how He brings streams in the desert. I was in a desert, right there in my hospital bed in the nursing home.

From that moment on, I began to get better. God's Word brought healing to my spirit and strength to my body. Soon I was walking with help. This was a miracle because the doctors had said I would probably never leave the nursing home.

God put special people in my life to help me through this difficult time. My wonderful husband made many sacrifices for me, always putting my needs first. A church where we had served for twelve years offered us a temporary home on their property and brought meals to my family while I was in the hospital and nursing home. I was truly blessed to have so many loving people surround me.

My daughter quit her job and her family moved in with us to help take care of me. Having my grandchildren with me was therapeutic. I would get in my wheelchair and race my little grandson on his bike outside. If my seven-month-old grandson was fussy, we would ride around in the house, or if he was sleepy, we would get in my wheelchair and ride outside until he fell asleep. My two grandsons were the best medicine I could ever have.

In 2010, the doctors gave me two weeks to live. Five years later, my life is almost back to normal. I can keep house, baby-sit my grandchildren, go on mission trips, and enjoy life with my family. Last Easter, I drove my car to church again for the first time. The small mass on my brain stem remains to this day, but has never affected me in any way. My multiple sclerosis is managed with medication. He has done a "new thing" in my life and in my body. My healing has been miraculous.

I hated leaving the Dominican Republic and the people we had come to love. However, I would not have missed seeing the power of God in our lives and the glory of God as we overcame the challenges we faced. Through the trials, I walked by faith, and God kept all His promises. Having Him at my side has made it a journey of joy and triumph!

# A Christmas Day Miracle

### by Beverly Sce

My dad was a plumber by trade and had his own heating and plumbing business. It was physically demanding at times, but Dad repeatedly told us how he liked to help people. He felt it was his calling in life.

One day in the early summer of 1968, while carrying a bathtub to a second floor bathroom, he injured his back and excruciating pain confined him to bed. After several doctors' appointments, there was still no definitive diagnosis. MRIs and CAT scans did not exist. One doctor diagnosed arthritis; another suggested back traction. My dad was really suffering; he was willing to try anything. He wanted and needed to get better. Dad was not able to work. No work meant no money and he had a family to support.

I remember each evening our angels of mercy, Uncle Moe and Uncle Ed, came over to help my dad get out of bed and walk him step by step from the bedroom to the bathroom. It was like a baby taking the first steps. I worried my dad would never get better. I worried he would never walk again by himself. How would my mom handle this with three children, ages four, seven, and twelve, and a bedridden husband to care for? However, in this time of trial, the Lord gave her extraordinary grace of strength and perseverance. Mom was a remarkable woman who handled it all with no complaint.

I recall my mom whispering to her sister Gerry on the telephone, "The doctors have to do something; Jack can't go on like this. We need a miracle." Maybe my young ears were not supposed to hear this, but it went from my lips straight to the ears of Jesus. I knew He would listen.

As I think back to that time, over forty years ago, the words of my mother echo in my mind. "I'm praying that your father gets well. If the good Lord makes him better, I will never ask for anything for myself in life." My mother was faithful to this promise throughout her life. When she passed away in 2010, I'm certain the good Lord rewarded her abundantly for her faithfulness.

Day after day, she assured Dad he would get better, walk again, and be able to go back to work. "Just have faith and pray," she repeated again and again.

A span of three months may not seem like much time, but to a child, this time of sickness seemed like forever. Dad remained confined to bed and unable to walk on his own. He was depressed and my mom begged the doctors to do something. I don't think the doctors knew what to do. It was 1968 and the technological advances for medical diagnosis were very limited.

I thought our miracle came in October 1968 when they finally diagnosed my dad with a herniated lumbar disc and he underwent surgery. The doctors said the surgery was successful, but Dad still could not walk without assistance. Was there an answer to this problem? Dad gave up any hope of getting well. He thought he would never walk again, but the Lord had a different plan.

Our family's faith was strong. We believed the Lord heard our prayers and would answer our plea for help. Christmas morning 1968, my dad followed his morning routine. I don't know how it began, but before my eyes, Dad walked from the bedroom, one small step at a time, toward the living room where the Christmas tree stood, shiny with tinsel and colored lights.

"Daddy's walking! Daddy's walking!" I hollered, standing with my younger sister in the hallway by our living room on Christmas morning. Tears ran down our cheeks as we repeated, "Daddy's walking! Daddy's walking!" Our piercing screams penetrated the early morning quiet as my mother frantically ran from the kitchen to see what was happening.

"Look, Mom, look. Daddy's walking. Santa Claus came and gave us the best Christmas present we ever got," I said.

"Santa didn't give us this present," Mom said. "Jesus did. He heard our prayers and He answered just like I told you He would. The good Lord has given us a Christmas miracle. That's why your Dad is walking."

It was our best Christmas ever. We had presents under the Christmas tree, but the best Christmas present of all was the miracle Jesus brought. Dad was able to walk without help. It was a gift our family never forgot. It was our Christmas Day miracle!

# To Live Again

## by Nanette Thorsen-Snipes

The rain slid down my windshield in rivulets and everything seemed blurry as I wiped away tears. The tractor-trailer had roared past me a half hour before, kicking up water as it sped by. I looked at my still trembling hands. They were red where I'd gripped the steering wheel. At once, I realized how close I had come to pulling in front of the truck.

"Oh, God," I whispered, "please help me." I had never felt so alone in my life. Even though I was remarried with two more children, a cat, and a dog, I felt completely alone and empty.

I stopped living—really living—on the Saturday after Thanksgiving in 1983. My second husband, Jim, and I had made an early morning grocery run. We'd just gotten home when my strapping fifteen-year-old son stopped me cold. His brown eyes were filled with pain, and swimming in tears. He tried to talk, but the words lodged in his throat.

"What's wrong?" I screamed. I shook his shoulders in desperation. Frightening words tumbled out. "Dad killed himself," he said.

*No! It can't be true!* My former husband was still young.

At forty, he had built another life with his second wife; he owned a beautiful house, had a good job—everything he could ask for. *No, it must be a horrible mistake.*

"Mom," my son said, "did you hear me?"

Memories seared my mind and somewhere in the deep recesses, I wondered, *Why?* I recalled the long-ago spring day in my bedroom with my lavender curtains fluttering in the breeze. I sat on the edge of the bed as my husband tossed clothes into a suitcase after I'd said I wanted a separation. I needed peace in my life as the endless screaming battles had exhausted me. I needed a separation because his anger and hostility terrified me. The kitchen walls attested to his anger with large holes the size of his fist.

While packing his clothes, he asked a question that chilled me. "You're really going to do it, aren't you? You're really going to leave."

A small voice I barely recognized as mine said, "Yes."

I was horrified to see him walk to the closet shelf and pull down the large black gun we'd bought for protection. He began inserting bullets into each chamber. I heard each one click and I measured my life in each one.

Tears dripped off my chin as the memory faded and the reality of his death set in. *Why?* The assurance of Jim's arm around me added comfort and softened the news. Memories of my former roller-coaster marriage faded back where it belonged—into the past. My mind couldn't contain the pain.

*How could he do this? How could he leave his children?* As that year turned into nine, the anger and pain consumed me. Soon, I found myself unable to concentrate. I couldn't remember to keep dentist or doctor appointments, names vanished, and I couldn't follow a simple recipe. Doing my laundry, if I could remember, was a huge task.

Once, Jim insisted I go to a family reunion, but I couldn't. It was more than I could handle. It took every ounce of strength just to make it to the next day.

"I can't go," I said softly.

"Sure you can," he said, trying to encourage me.

I began screaming inside. *I can't go! Don't you understand? Aren't you even listening to me?* In minutes, the rage I'd bottled up for years, exploded, and I began weeping uncontrollably.

"I think you'd better see a counselor," Jim said.

I shook my head, wiping away tears with the back of my hand. "I'll be all right."

This last emotional event brought me to the side of the road a week later. As I crossed over the expressway on my way home from the doctor's office, I saw a tractor-trailer bearing down on me. *It would be so easy. It would be over in just a few moments. All I had to do was swerve in front of the truck.*

The truck rumbled toward my car, its back wheels kicking up water. I gripped the steering wheel. *All I have to do is pull into its path.* My breath caught in my throat. As I allowed the truck to pass, it rattled my car. I pulled over. *What is wrong with me?* I put my car in park with the motor still running.

I watched a lightning bolt arc across the sky and the clouds crack open. Raindrops pelted my windshield. I let the tears flow.

"Oh, God," I prayed, "please help me."

I sat there for what seemed an eternity. As the rain slowed, I saw sunshine slicing through the clouds. A beginning peace began in my heart, and I could almost feel an inner Voice remind me, "My grace is sufficient for you, for my power is made perfect in weakness."

As the biblical message sank in, I knew what had to be done. With my newfound strength, I called a Christian counselor. After several years of counseling, I was relieved to know that my thoughts of suicide were merely cries for help.

One day after I had begun rising early for devotions, I read in the Bible that I was a child of God, and He loved me very much. I could barely fathom such love, but on a human level that was how much my husband loved me.

Jim loved me enough to stand by me as I dealt with the loss of my former husband. He went with me to counseling, week after week, sharing my pain and anguish. He even offered to go with me to the gravesite to say a final goodbye—a moment of forgiving, of releasing the hurt and anger inside. The pain was so great that I never physically made it to his grave. However, in my mind, I imagined standing in front of his headstone and saying once and forever, "I'm sorry."

Sometime later, I was up at daybreak to watch the sun rise. I poured coffee and walked to my back porch swing. Warming my hands on the mug, I marveled at the first rays of light. I sat there a long time, wondering what had happened to the years the locusts had eaten.

Unlike the rainy day I sat in my car trembling, I was alive for the first time in years. I watched vibrant colors of lavender and pink filter across the sky as the sun blinked above the horizon. The back door groaned open, and I shared the day's beauty with Jim as he sat down beside me.

He put his arm around me and gently squeezed my shoulder. I felt the soft touch of a breeze playing in my hair.

*My grace is sufficient for you.* My heart leapt with joy at the closeness of the Lord's presence.

I closed my eyes, and I thanked Him.

This story was originally published in
*Miracles and Tough Times*, Guidepost Books, 2008.

# The Gentle Giant

## by Nikki Spearman with Lee Spearman

Lee thought it was a normal ending of a Christmas tree season until late afternoon when he started feeling sick. He was glad the season was over because he was exhausted after several twelve-hour days of hard work. His arm was swollen and the pain was intense. He felt terrible. It was too late to see a doctor, but he needed treatment so he'd have to go to the emergency room.

He showered at my mother's house, but was too weak to dry off. Mom called me, "Nikki, I think you need to come … Lee is really sick!"

He insisted on driving himself to the nearest hospital and checked into the ER for what he thought was probably a broken arm and the flu. The doctor sent him by ambulance to the regional medical center for critical care. In the ambulance, he went into shock and stopped breathing, but the EMT resuscitated him. When he arrived at the hospital, his blood pressure was 50/20.

Lee pleaded with me before getting into the ambulance, "Please don't leave me." I didn't. I stayed with him for forty days—until I got the flu. I visited him at every opportunity—

talking, praying, rubbing his head, and singing to him. When I became too sick to stay with him, our son Tom took off from his job to take care of his Dad. Tom remained at Lee's bedside until he finished rehab and came home.

After numerous tests, doctors determined that a bacterial infection was ravaging Lee's body, but no one knew what kind of infection or the source. He had septic poisoning and his body was shutting down.

The doctors told me to gather the family together and plan for Christmas without Lee because there was a good chance that he would not be with us for Christmas. I was devastated! This was inconceivable to me. I refused to believe it! It felt like we were in a bad dream, and I had to do something to get us out of it.

I moved into the waiting room of the intensive care unit, sleeping on the couch and visiting Lee every hour or two depending on his status. The nearest restroom became a refuge. There I had many conversations with God. Understanding was difficult; blame was pointless; negotiations proved futile. I even thought Christmas in heaven might be exactly what Lee would want. Finally, I stopped praying for Lee's recovery and simply prayed for peace in my heart.

They put Lee on the ventilator in a medically induced coma. After eleven days, the doctors told me Lee's organs had started to shut down. Due to a fever of 107° off and on for twenty-four hours, they told me he probably had brain damage that would cause memory loss if he did wake up and recover.

The doctors made a decision to remove Lee from the ventilator and perform a tracheotomy. Several nurses and doctors were in the room to assist with the procedure. When they turned the ventilator off, Lee made an audible sigh—a single breath—and hope was restored. The doctors and I expressed disbelief. The medical staff shared my tears of joy. All the nurses and doctors were amazed and said it was a Christmas Eve Miracle.

Our family celebrated Christmas without Lee in a family room at the children's hospital next door. Close friends and family members purchased gifts for our children and provided food for the event. The outpouring of love was overwhelming.

Because Lee's blood pressure was so dangerously low, they gave him medications called vasopressors to keep his heart beating and his brain functioning. Vasopressors forced blood to his vital organs causing lack of blood flow to his extremities. In Lee's situation though, these medications were life-saving. However, they also resulted in dead tissue in his hands and feet. His muscles deteriorated and he faced the reality of losing his hands and feet. I knew this would change all our lives forever.

A month after Lee entered the hospital, our five adopted children visited their daddy for the first time. The next day Lee underwent bi-lateral, below the knee amputation. At this point, his internal organs started to recover. Over the next several weeks, Lee had several surgeries and lost multiple digits on each hand. In spite of all this, we were ecstatic that Lee was still with us.

After the amputations, Lee went to the rehab center. Many doctors, nurses, and technicians worked with him. They watched with amazement at how hard he worked and the progress he made. The medical staff couldn't believe it! Even the local newspaper came to talk with Lee and the medical staff. They decided to write a series of articles about the 6' 2", 260-pound "Gentle Giant." After 82 days of God's amazing love, Lee came home to us with all his organs working and no brain damage from the spiking fever.

Our first miracle was Lee's recovery, but others followed. During rehab, AP news picked up Lee's story and it went viral. A couple from Georgia heard about Lee and drove all the way to Wilmington, NC to bring Lee a handicap van that was just right for our family of seven. The man said the van had belonged to his brother who had passed away, and the family wanted to give it to someone who really needed it. All he asked in return was that Lee and I keep in touch.

Donations poured in as the word spread about Lee's illness and miraculous recovery. With that money, friends and family were able to make the house handicap accessible and build a ramp for his wheelchair.

Lee remained in the wheelchair until he mastered walking with his prosthetic legs. Now he can drive the van, play with the children again, go swimming, and speak at churches that ask him to share his testimony.

Lee is so thankful for the thoughtful, kind things people did to help our family during this time. Without his faith, family, and friends, Lee says, "I know I never would have made it!"

Today Lee closed the Christmas tree lot again. He has come full circle because of the love and prayers of a multitude of people scattered around the world and the amazing grace of our Heavenly Father.

Ann White Knowles

126

# Twenty-One Days

**by JoAnn Reno Wray**

Monday, July 2, 1990 was a typical sunny summer afternoon. My husband Roger mowed the front yard. Our daughter, Amie got ready for work. Son, Mike, age 18, rooted in his less than neat room. I folded a basket of laundry in the living room. Nothing foretold the storm about to hit our lives.

Five minutes later, Mike joined me in the living room. He stood, waiting. Finally, he said, "Mom, I think I might need to see a doctor."

"Why is that?" I asked, unconcerned.

"Um. It's kind of embarrassing." He choked out.

I focused fully on him. "Honey, you know you can talk to me or Dad about anything. Just tell me."

During his last few months of high school he'd had many physical problems, had fainted several times, and fought increased headaches and pain. His hands had constant tremors. He'd also totaled our only car driving to his graduation ceremony, yet walked away with only minor injuries. The week after graduation, he'd taken a canoe float trip with friends. The canoe tipped over trapping Mike underneath, nearly drowning him. He'd survived all that, what could possibly be that bad now?

Mike fidgeted, then whispered. "My left testicle is way bigger than the right. It hurts. Something's wrong."

I dropped a towel in the basket, momentarily speechless. I asked, "Do you want Dad to look at it?" Mike nodded his head yes, as frightened tears filled his eyes. "You can wait in your room, I'll get Dad."

Soon Roger stood in the living room, his face bloodless. "We need to call the doctor—now. I don't know what's wrong, but he needs a doctor." Then he added, "Maybe he hurt himself in the canoe accident?"

Mike's appointment was 9:00 a.m. the next morning so we dropped Roger off at work, then drove to the doctor's office. I can still see the alarm on Doctor Van Schoyck's face after Mike's exam. The world suddenly tilted upside down. What was happening?

Doctor Van sent us to x-ray. When we returned, he gravely informed us that Mike needed go to the urologist's office immediately. I struggled to be brave, holding back my tears. Mike was shell-shocked, clinging fiercely to my hand. I called Roger and a friend brought him to the urologist's office.

There, Mike endured another exam before the urologist sent him to join us in the waiting room while he studied the x-rays. Fifteen minutes later a receptionist ushered us into the doctor's office and closed the door. We sat in the chairs lined up in front of the doctor's desk. A lump the size of Alaska lodged in my throat. Roger held one of Mike's hands; I held the other. We prayed quietly while waiting.

Soon the door banged open making us jump and the doctor marched in. He plopped in his chair, then, without preamble, said, "Mike has testicular cancer. His left testicle is four times normal size due to the tumor. Typically, there's an eighty per cent chance of recovery. However, he'll need more tests before we can determine that. He needs surgery immediately to remove the tumor and testicle. Do you want the surgery Thursday or Friday? Talk it over and I'll come back shortly."

"Dear Jesus, help us, please heal Mike!" my husband choked out. We both stood and hugged Mike fiercely, all of us crying.

We scheduled the surgery for Friday, determined to enjoy July 4th as a family, just as always. We called our family and church friends, and asked them to pray. That Friday, Mike had surgery and stayed overnight at the hospital.

After surgery, Mike went through more tests and CT scans. Each time we saw the urologist or other doctors, Mike's chances of survival decreased. He was finally referred to an oncologist, Dr. Vicki Baker, at St. John's Hospital / La Fortune Cancer Center in Tulsa, OK. We learned the cancer had spread to all Mike's lymph nodes, caused six tumors the size of a large man's fist in his lower abdomen, and thirty-six spots of cancer the size of a quarter or larger on his lungs. The oncologist quietly told us Mike's chances of survival were less than twenty per cent because the cancer had not been found early and was very fast growing. Later, she told us that he'd actually had almost no chance of survival, but she had wanted us to have hope.

On July 16, 1990, Mike was admitted to the hospital for his first five-day round of chemotherapy. He received three chemotherapy and four blocker drugs, to control side effects, administered intravenously for four hours daily.

Mike lay in the bed weak and frail, while I sat in a chair or walked the room, singing praises to God or praying for Mike's healing. Roger joined us each evening. There was nothing else we could do for him. Our baby was in pain, fighting for his life. It was agonizing.

Soon the week was over. Mike had done so well that in twenty-one days, for his next week of chemo, he could have it as an out-patient. For five days, he went to the cancer center, and took his four-hour treatment.

Those twenty-one days passed in a blur. Most of Mike's hair fell out, even his eye lashes. The day the barber buzzed the remaining hair off his head was especially hard for me. He came home, struck a pose in the doorway, and announced, "I've launched a new hair style – the Jean Luc Picard of the Star Ship Enterprise look." I ran in the bathroom and stuffed a towel in my mouth to mute my sobs. Here was my son, sense of humor still intact, still fighting the good fight.

During Mike's outpatient chemo, my parents came from

Ohio to spend time with Mike. They drove us back and forth daily for his chemo.

The first thing Mike did that initial out-patient day was have more x-rays. We waited nervously in the waiting room for that and while Mike's blood was drawn to check cancer markers. Soon, the nurse called us to the exam room.

Mom and I walked in and saw Mike in a gown, feet swinging back and forth, his bald head shining under the harsh lights. Mom immediately gave Mike a huge bear hug. "I love you, you know?" she said. He nodded, grinned, and hugged her back.

A few minutes passed before Doctor Vicki arrived. She was all business, shaking hands with us. Then she announced, "I wanted you to see the x-rays taken before Mike started chemotherapy." She slapped the films on the light board, flicking the switch.

I stood behind, to her right as she pointed out and explained the images. I stole glances at Mike wondering how in the world all that cancer could possibly be in his skinny, six foot- one inch frame. My heart cried, *Please Jesus let me have the cancer so Mike doesn't have to go through this.*

Immediately, God's loving voice echoed in my heart, *But, my daughter, that is done already. I looked down from heaven and saw the cancer of sin killing my children, making them ill, separating them from my own heart. So I sent my son, Jesus, to carry that sin and bring healing by the stripes he bore at*

*Calvary.* I felt my fear and tension dissolve.

I gulped when I realized the doctor was crying. I could only imagine more bad news even after God's comforting words. I said, "Please, just tell me, so we know how to pray. God is Mike's healer!"

She turned, snatched off her glasses, and said, "It's okay. I've just never seen a miracle! Look at the x-rays from today!"

She quickly mounted the new films, explaining each as she did. The large tumors in Mike's lower abdomen had shrunk by sixty per cent. I blinked hard, watching the doctor point to the x-ray of Mike's chest. All thirty-six cancerous spots on his lungs were totally gone. Additionally, she told us, the markers in his blood had fallen radically.

Dr. Baker hugged me tightly, then announced, "Chemotherapy never works in twenty-one days, but Jesus does!"

I laughed and cried with joy as my mother hugged the stuffing out of Mike, shouting, "You're going to live!"

Live he did! Almost twenty-five years have passed. Mike remains a living example of God's healing touch. Now married to Grace, their son won an appointment to the Naval Academy in 2014. Mike assists with praise and worship, plus teaching and preaching God's word at a Chinese Baptist church. No pronouncement of sparse survival odds by doctors could stop that. Twenty-one days or twenty-one years, Father God is ever on the scene with miracles daily.

# Christmas Presence

**by Diana C. Derringer**

*Serenity is not freedom from the storm,*
*but peace amid the storm.*
~ S. A. Jefferson-Wright

"We've scheduled your husband's heart procedure for tomorrow. As soon as we complete his discharge papers, the ambulance will take him to Louisville. If all goes as planned, he should be transferred to the rehabilitation hospital the following day."

Although Christmas was only four days away, I embraced that incredible news.

Our family had gone from the doctor saying, "We can't ever say there's no hope, but it doesn't look good," on December 10, 2009, to witnessing unbelievable recovery in the days that followed. A heart attack, stroke, fall resulting in a severe brain injury, and lack of oxygen from an extended period with no heart or lung function, plus a 2004 diagnosis of a malignant brain tumor—any one of those alone could result in death. But all together, death is almost guaranteed. Almost.

A surgeon friend, in the same Sunday school class as my husband, was on duty when my husband entered the emergency room. He volunteered to meet with the family. Not one to hold back bad news, he shared the numbers indicating almost no brain activity. We could remove the respirator immediately or wait. He anticipated no difference in the ultimate results.

My husband had said for years he never wanted his life prolonged by artificial means and had signed a medical directive to that effect. However, we chose to wait until we saw a cardiologist.

This decision followed group prayer with two of our pastors, two family members, and two close friends. As each person prayed, God's love and our love for one another filled the room. With tears streaming, I thanked God for time with my husband, prayed for healing, and expressed thanks for whatever the future held. I acknowledged the superiority of God's love over my own and placed my trust in that love.

Friends from church and community quietly came and went, praying, hugging, and loving. Family members arrived for what we thought were final goodbyes. One at a time, they held my husband's hand, talked to him, and shared their love.

When the staff moved him from the emergency room, the waiting area quickly filled. My sister remained in the room with me through the night. I held my husband's hand and silently prayed, not so much with words as with my heart.

Around 3:00 a. m., the reality that he might die in a few hours hit full force. I lowered my head against the bed rail and sobbed. Within minutes, God flooded my soul with His presence. I learned later that a friend awoke around 3:00 a. m., so burdened she couldn't sleep. Although she prayed for my husband, she focused on my need for comfort and strength.

Near dawn, my husband's arm moved around my waist. Although he had exhibited involuntary movement earlier, this felt different. It felt deliberate. And I thanked God for that moment.

Later in the day, when the doctor removed the ventilator, my husband breathed on his own, tracked motion and sounds with his eyes, and responded with hand squeezes to questions. Within another twenty-four hours he was sitting up, talking, and soon making jokes. The surgeon, who uses such language sparingly, stated quite openly, "Well, it looks like we have us a miracle." The cardiologist, who didn't see us again until the following week, charted the little known medical word, "Wow!"

My husband's new nickname, *the miracle man*, quickly spread throughout the hospital, our church, and the community.

The day EMS loaded him for the hospital transfer, I made a beeline home to pack our essentials for the next few weeks. After I gathered clothing, personal items, and reading and writing supplies, I realized we had to celebrate Christmas too. So I grabbed a small crocheted Christmas tree and a miniature nativity scene. Satisfied the two were perfect for the days ahead, I added what Christmas gifts I'd purchased before all the excitement.

The next day's news could not have been better. I nodded as the doctors talked and pointed. A short time later, we prepared for our final transfer.

Most that I packed from home remained in the car until my husband was successfully settled in the rehabilitation hospital the next afternoon. Since they had extra bed space during the holidays, they approved my request to move into the room with him. I was firmly convinced this was vital for my husband's mental, physical, and emotional recovery, plus my own sense of well-being. I told them, "He's lost both long- and short-term memory, and I'm his memory bank. I need to be there to help him review the past and verify the accuracy of any recall."

In addition, his weak muscles and poor balance placed him at increased risk for another fall. In spite of a bed alarm, he could quickly hit the floor before staff reached him. I never had to present that argument. It spoke for itself immediately after our arrival. When a worker escorted me to his room, he wasn't there. While she asked other staff, "Where's Mr. Derringer?" I checked the bathroom door. Left briefly unattended, he somehow made it to the bathroom alone, a terrifying way to begin his stay.

Above all, I believed in the healing power of love. He needed to know that he wasn't in this battle alone. I wanted to offer as much normalcy as possible ... to touch him and tell him "I love you" several times a day ... to eat and sleep with him

… to talk, read, and watch TV together … and to pester the daylights out of him when he grew weary of all the hard work ahead.

So we began our daily routine of physical, occupational, and speech therapy. I reinforced the staff's efforts, using their suggestions. When I included additional ideas from our seasoned speech therapist sister-in-law, the young hospital therapist applauded our efforts and added them to her bag of tricks. The hospital schedule proved extremely taxing for both of us, but we knew immediate, intensive therapy resulted in faster and more successful recovery.

During free time, my husband often slept. His body needed that extra rest for maximum healing. We also looked at family pictures and tried to remember names. We talked about the recent and not so recent past and how everyone fit into it. We discussed his employment history. We relived our favorite vacations. We brought the past into the present—over and over again.

Although separated by several miles, friends and relatives continued to make brief, well-spaced visits. A few joined us Christmas Eve and Christmas day. Siblings helped fill in the gaps of gifts not yet purchased and made deliveries for us.

But we also had several hours alone every day. During that time, I found myself gazing at our tiny tree and nativity scene. In spite of the challenges we'd faced, and those that lay ahead, my heart overflowed with the blessings we'd received.

In a half joking, half serious way, I told a few late visitors, "I've learned that all a person really needs is enough to eat, a warm place to sleep, and someone to love."

Our solitude also provided time to contemplate anew the significance of Christmas and the gift of love and life offered to our world. So I gave thanks. Thanks that we were together. Thanks that we had abundant medical and emotional support. Thanks for a warm, comfortable place to stay until we could return home. Greater still, thanks that, because of God's Presence on Earth that night so long ago, we would never have to face the future alone.

This story originally appeared in *LIVE*, December 2013 and in *Christian Devotions* 2014.

# UPDATE:

My husband and I have celebrated Christmas at home rather than in a hospital every year since 2009. Although he continues to experience residual effects from the brain tumor, heart attack, stroke, and brain injury, his progress astounds medical professionals. We have also had countless opportunities to share God's love with others as a result of our difficulties. Every day, whatever the opportunity, whatever the difficulty, we give thanks for the extraordinary presence of God.

# The Red Shirt

**by Ann White Knowles**

I had just arrived home from school; I could hear the phone ringing as I hurried into the house.

"Hello---Oh, Beth, it's you. Is everything okay?

"Yes, calm down, Mama. I'm fine. I just need to talk to you a minute.

"Good. You've never called me from Turkey and with your due date this month. . . well, I was scared. But why are you calling me now?

"Mama, do you remember when we got married, you told me I would never go so far away that you wouldn't go to me if I needed you?"

Of course, I remembered that. I told all my children that when they left home. Wouldn't any mother do that? We live in a mobile world, a world very different from the one I grew up in in the 50s. And if my child needs me, I'm going to get to them somehow!

"Yes, I remember, Beth."

"Well, I need you to come to Turkey, Mama. This baby is due any day now; my best friend is in the states on leave, and Ron can't take off from work to stay home and take care of

Nicole. She is just eighteen months and I have no one to care
for her when I go to the hospital Can you and Cindy come and
stay for a few weeks until I'm on my feet again?"

Yes, honey, I'll go. You can count on your Mama just like
I told you.

"Try not to worry, Mama. All the signs over here are in
English and Turkish. You'll be just fine. There will people
everywhere to help you through customs and to change
planes."

"Okay, I'll call you back when I know our schedule. See
you soon! Love you. Bye now."

I hung up the phone with trembling hands. Turkey was so
far away from North Carolina! I had traveled the world with
Beth's father, but things were different since his death. I had
never flown by myself. I couldn't imagine getting on a plane
by myself and flying across the world to where she was. But I
knew I had to do it! We started making plans about when we
would leave.

Cindy had graduated from high school three months ago,
but she had a job and would have to get someone to work in
her place. We'd fly out of Raleigh/Durham on August 7, my
birthday.

So much to do! Such a long time to stay! Cindy had never
flown before and I could not let her know how nervous I was
about this trip. I reached out to where I found my strength--in

the Lord. I prayed long and hard every day as we prepared to leave for Incirlik, Turkey.

We flew from RDU airport to New York. Lines were long. The plane we boarded in New York was three stories high. We had to wait for an electrical storm to pass before we could take off. I had never seen a plane so big. It didn't seem like anything that big would be able to fly across the Atlantic.

We arrived in Istanbul, Turkey early in the morning. It was the end of our international flight; we would have to change to a Turkish airline to go on to Incirlik. We came through customs and never saw one word of English. The line led us out to an open area where everyone hustled to get to their next flight. We stood there and looked around, wondering which way to go.

Suddenly, from out of nowhere came a voice, "Hey, young lady, are you from Goldsboro, NC. I saw your red shirt! I used to work in Goldsboro. What are you doing here in Turkey? Where are you going? Can I help you get to your next plane?"

Coincidence? No way! God had sent us help just when we needed it most. On the back of Cindy's red shirt: Southern Wayne High School, Class of 1990, and a list of her graduating class.

We explained our story to him and he called his valet, "Come here, please. These ladies need our help. Take them to the plane to Incirlik and help them board. Be sure they have all their luggage."

We wanted to embrace him and tell him how much we appreciated his help, but he was gone as quickly as he had come. We settled onto the plane and awaited takeoff. Three hours later we were reunited with my daughter's family … tears of joy at seeing her and my little granddaughter again. We marveled at how God had taken care of us in such an amazing way as we traveled 12,000 miles across the US, the Atlantic, and Europe.

A week later my grandson was born. We spent three weeks with my daughter and her family. It seemed strange that we kept meeting military people from the Goldsboro area. And every time it was because Cindy was wearing a shirt from somewhere in North Carolina that people recognized..

Soon it would be time to return home. What then? Despite how God had helped us get to Incirlik, I was nervous about getting back to the States. No need to worry! God had everything under control. The daughter of the school principal in Incirlik was visiting her family over the summer, and she would be returning to the states the same day we were scheduled to fly out. Penny assured us we had nothing to worry about, that she would see us through all the airports on the way home.

On the day of our departure, we were excited to be going home and confident that all would be well since we'd be traveling with a college student who spent every summer with her family in Incirlik.

We hugged everyone and said our goodbyes, showering them with our tears; leaving the grandchildren was hard. We flew out of Incirlik late in the evening and arrived in Istanbul in the night.

Going through customs on the way out of Turkey was simple because we had not purchased anything to bring home with us. But we lost our college student; Penny was detained in customs; her visa had expired. She would not be allowed to continue the journey until she could get the visa renewed. However, we felt secure enough because it was our last flight out and the next stop we'd be back in the United States.

As I sat on the plane and waited for takeoff, I remembered all those Bible verses that reassured me of God's unfailing love.

For the eyes of the LORD roam to and fro over all the earth, to show Himself strong on behalf of those whose heart is fully devoted to Him (2 Chronicles 16:9).

Be still and know that I am God (Psalm 46:10).

I will never leave you or forsake you (Deuteronomy 31:8).

There was never any need for me to be anxious; He had us covered at all times.

# Ever Present God

## A poem by Diana Derringer

There are times in our lives when
the pain is so great,
the sorrow so intense,
the confusion so overwhelming
that we think we cannot possibly endure.

Yet, in those very moments
God's love can be so real,
His presence so unmistakable,
and His peace so calming.

He offers to wrap us
in arms of peace,
fill us with an everlasting joy,
and shower us with unconditional love.

God is simply waiting
to enter our lives,
to forgive us our failures,
and to give us hope.

Our difficulties may remain,
but we no longer have to carry them alone.
God will not leave.
He will not fail.
God is ever present God.

"The Lord himself goes before you and will be with you; he
will never leave you nor forsake you. Do not be afraid; do not
be discouraged" (Deuteronomy 31:8).

This poem was previously published.

# Contributors

**Lorna Bius,** a South Georgia girl at heart, currently lives in Denver, CO where she serves as the West Region LoveLoud Catalyst with the North American Mission Board. Lorna surrendered to ministry while attending Valdosta State University and has led student ministry at three churches and with the Nevada Baptist Convention in Women's and Community Ministry.

**Rebeca F. DePra** is a stay at home mother to three, author of *Hospitality in a Nutroll* (2009) and founder of W. A. L. T. (Write a Letter Today) a ministry that promotes a W.A.L.T. Day for children and adults to write hand-written letters for our American Heroes (our military personnel overseas)

**Diana Derringer,** a former social worker and adjunct professor, writes for several publications. She and her husband love to travel and serve as a friendship family to international students at the university. Visit her at www.dianaderringer.com.

**Natalie Driggs** is a pastor's wife, mother to three, and an ESL teacher. Her passion is missions and with her missionary heart, she reaches out to internationals here at home and on the mission field. She enjoys relaxing at the beach, walking her dog in the park, and communicating online with missionaries in faraway places.

**Eva Marie Everson** is the multiple award-winning, best-selling author of works, both fiction and non-fiction. In June 2015, Tyndale released her long-awaited novel, *Five Brides,* based on a true event. Eva Marie lives in Florida with her huggy-hubby and a dog that owns her.

**Rebecca K. Floyd** is a stay-at-home mom of Carolyn, age 12, and Franklin, age 7, with a husband who travels away from home during the week. Her son Franklin was born with a rare genetic mutation that caused his cancer and a separate progressive renal disease. Rebecca is also a Licensed Professional Counselor and a Stephen Minister in her church.

**Phyllis Q. Freeman** has been a freelance writer for twenty years, publishing more than four hundred devotionals, magazine articles, and newspaper human interest stories. She lives near Chattanooga, Tennessee and is published in *Chicken Soup for the Soul: Answered Prayers,* and *Angel in Uniform.* Phyllis teaches classes on inspirational writing and writes devotions for three publishing houses.

**Martha P. Hales** grew up on a farm near Sanford, NC. She studied Early Childhood Education at Campbell College and then married her roommate's brother. She is the mother of three and grandmother of five. She has always been involved in her church, mostly in women's ministry and music. She plays the organ and piano.

**Linda Harris** has been a freelance writer and editor for over thirty years. She is a member of The Christian PEN (Proofreaders and Editors' Network) and The Christian Editor Connection. Visit her at **www.PerfectWordEditing.com**

**Kevin Johnson** was born in Weatherford, TX. After spending his childhood living in New York, Virginia, North Carolina, and Iowa, he and his wife Tracie settled in Athens, TX where they reside today, raising their three children, KayLyn, Kinlie, and Tyler.

**Ann White Knowles** is a writer, editor, and teacher, and has a heart for missions and adult literacy. She is author of three published books, *Teaching Reading in Adult Basic Education*, *Fifty Years of Literacy Missions in North Carolina*, and *The Extraordinary Presence of God*. Find her at www.Write-Pathway.com

**Jeanette E. Levellie** "Nuttie with a dash of meat" best describes this wife of one, mother of two, grandmother of three, and waitress to four cats. Jeanette has published columns, articles, stories, and two inspirational books: *Two Scoops of Grace with Chuckles on Top* and *The Heart of Humor*. Find her at www.jeanettelevellie.com

**J. Martin, aka Judy Martin-Urban,** loves to write non-fiction and fiction (Christian fiction as Jude Urbanski). She has published three books, is part of an anthology, and writes inspirational articles for Maximum Living Magazine. Her passions are nature, people and places. Visit Judy at www.judeurbanski.com.

**Maggie Matthews** is the mother of four and grandmother of seven. Missions are her passion and she uses her writing to advance the cause of Christ. She wants her words to touch the hearts of her readers and make a difference in their lives.

**Joy E. Miller** lives in Virginia. She has published in "The Upper Room," "Christian Devotions," and "Inspired Women." She enjoys reading, journaling and writing notes of encouragement. Joy is passionate about pro-life issues.

**Ane Mulligan** writes Southern-fried fiction served with a tall, sweet iced tea. She's a novelist, a humor columnist, and a multi-published playwright. She resides in Sugar Hill, GA, with her artist husband and two dogs of Biblical proportion. You can find her at **www.anemulligan.com**

**Patricia "Trish" Nixon** and her three children have collectively shared the Gospel of Jesus Christ in twelve nations. She has received numerous poetry awards and published one book regarding her mission experiences: *I Left My Father's House . . . I Left My Father's Land.* A former resident of Buffalo, NY, she now resides in Florida.

**Julie H. Pickern,** former missionary to the Dominican Republic, has but one passion—to tell people about Jesus and the amazing things He's done in her life. She loves spending time with her children and grandchildren and going back to the Dominican Republic on mission trips.

**Claudia Russell** and her husband have four children and four grandchildren. They have served as foster parents and house parents for Baptist Children's Homes. She worked as church secretary and after retirement went back to serve as Financial Secretary at Love Memorial Baptist Church in Goldsboro, NC. She has a heart for missions and a love for people.

**Beverly Sce,** Ph.D., R.N., is an author and accomplished quilter. Beverly lives with her husband in Bucks County, PA. She has had a long career in Public Health Administration. As founder/Director of Jesus Divine Mercy Ministry, she is a sought after inspirational speaker for retreats and conferences. Beverly loves to hear from her readers at **beverlysce@comcast.net**.

**Nanette Thorsen-Snipes** has published articles, columns, devotions, and reprints in more than forty publications and sixty compilation books, including stories and devotions in Guideposts anthologies in the Miracles series: The New Women's Devotional Bible, and Chicken Soup, among others. She and her husband have four grown children and eight grandchildren. Website: **www.faithworkseditorial.com** Contact **nsnipes@bellsouth.net**.

**Nicole Spearman and Lee Spearman** have been married 29 years and most of that time they have been involved in children and family ministry. They have adopted eight children, five of whom are still at home. Their hearts and their home have always had a special place for troubled children.

**Sherry Willetts** is a multi-gifted woman with a servant's heart. She is mother to four, grandmother to six, and caregiver for her husband. She sings in the choir and works in many areas at her church. She loves country living and enjoys interior design when time permits.

**JoAnn Reno Wray** writings have been published over 3500 times in print and web periodicals and included in more than sixteen book compilations. She's also served as a speaker/teacher for local and national writer conferences.

# About the Author

Ann Knowles is a writer, editor, and teacher who wants her words to make a difference in people's lives. She has published locally, nationally, and internationally—articles, devotions, and biblical radio dramas.

Her passions are missions and writing. A retired teacher, she enjoys teaching at writers' conferences and speaking to church and civic groups. Ann and her husband Stan live in southeastern North Carolina. She's a real Carolina girl, loves watermelon, sand between her toes, and sweet iced tea.

She earned her M.A. Ed. at East Carolina University and has done graduate studies in religious journalism and missions at Southeaster Seminary. Find Ann at:

**Website: www.writepathway.com**

**Blog: www.annknowles.blogspot.com**

**LinkedIn: www.linkedin.com/pub/ann-white-knowles/16/963/67as**

**Facebook: www.facebook.com/ann.whiteknowles**

# Note from Ann

The stories in this book are true and factual as the authors remember them. Minor details in a few of the stories have been changed to protect the innocent, and some authors chose to write under a pseudonym.

Pastors often use this starfish story as a sermon illustration: Two little girls walking along the beach encountered hundreds of starfish washed ashore as the last tide receded. If the starfish were not returned to the water long before the next high tide, they would die on the beach.

With a concerned heart, desiring to save some, one of the girls began picking up the starfish and throwing them back into the ocean.

"What good is that?" the other girl asked." Don't you know we can't save all these starfish before the tide comes in?"

Undeterred, the first little girl picked up another starfish, threw it into the ocean, and said, "Well, at least I can make a difference for that one!"

Your story may not make a difference to everyone who reads it, but it will make a difference to the one God wants to read it. Isaiah 12:4 says *Thank the Lord! Praise his name! Tell the world what he has done. Oh, how mighty he is! (NLB)* Telling your story puts life in this Scripture. Your story is a reminder that God has done something wonderful in your life.

Every story will make a difference to someone. If God has done something special in your life, you have a story to tell, and God will put the story in the hands of the person who needs it. Be faithful and tell your story every chance you get in order that people may be blessed and God's name glorified.

**Thank you
for reading our books!**

**Look for other books**

**published by**

www.TMPbooks.com